PULPIT DIAGRAMS

WITH BRIEF NOTES OF EXPLANATION

Z. T. SWEENEY, Editor

GOSPEL ADVOCATE COMPANY

NASHVILLE, TENNESSEE

1958

INTRODUCTION

THE appeal to the eye has long been recognized as no less potent than the appeal to the ear in the proclamation of truth. Hence, the use of sermon charts and diagrams has become a popular method of presenting the message of salvation. Evangelists and ministers serving local congregations alike have used such sermons to the profit and edification of their hearers.

In issuing a new edition of Pulpit Diagrams, the publishers have every reason to believe that this justly popular work will meet with the same cordial reception which was accorded it when it first appeared. It is safe to say that no other book of the kind has ever made a greater appeal to the pulpit at large. The author, whose fame as an evangelist and lecturer is international, has selected his material with the greatest care, and has produced a volume which is available to the busy minister. Few books contain so much thought packed into such a brief compass. Every page is condensed, and there is no padding. The forty-eight sermons to be found in this volume are all upon themes of transcendent interest and cover the whole field of Christian doctrine and experience.

It is with unusual pleasure that we send forth this book upon what we feel sure will be a career of renewed service in the Master's name.

TABLE OF CONTENTS

I.—RELATION, PREPARATION, ETC.

JESUS CHRIST is the author of the Christian religion, and the founder, foundation and finisher of the Christian Church. While in the world, he, with inerrant wisdom, taught men of "the things pertaining to the kingdom of God." When he left the world he gave the apostles authority to teach for him, and gave them the wisdom that made their teaching as infallible as his own. Whatever, then, is taught by Christ or the apostles is "an end of all controversy" with those who believe in the divine nature of Jesus Christ. In his teaching, and in that of his apostles, the method most used is the illustrative. They took of the relations of life already existing among men to teach us the nature of that new relation which Christ died to establish between men and God. In this diagram I have chosen some of these relations, and wish to note their bearing upon the new relation which they are intended, in some of its features at least, to illustrate.

To this end I call your attention to the first column of the diagram—that of "RELATION." 1. In John xv. 5, we have a vine and its branches. 2. Heb. xii. 1, we have a race and its runners. 3. II. Tim. ii. 4, we have an army and its soldiers. 4. Eph. ii. 19, we have a government and its citizens. 5. Rom. vii. 4, we have matrimony and its bride. 6. Rom. viii. 16, we have a family and its children. Now, the purpose of these is to teach us that Christ came to establish a new relation in the world. This relation I have designated in the diagram by the word "CHURCH." If I have chosen the right word, the church must possess, in some sense, the characteristics of all these other relations. It does—for the church is a vine and its branches; a race and its runners; an army with its Captain and soldiers; a government with its Ruler and citizens; a marriage with its Bridegroom and bride, and a family with its Father and children.

Passing from the column of relation to that of "PREPARATION," we notice, in regard to each of these relations, there is a state of preparation necessary to its enjoyment. 1. The branch must be "trimmed" before it enters the vine. 2. The runner must "train" before entering the race. 3. The soldier must be "interested" before he enters the army. 4. The alien must "desire" before he enters the government. 5. The woman must "love" before entering wedlock. 6. The child must be "generated" before entering the family. Now, all this teaches us that there is some state of preparation necessary and antecedent to membership in the church. In the diagram I have this state of preparation designated by the word "Faith." I mean neither more nor less by this term than Jesus means when he says, "He that *believeth* and is baptized shall be saved," or than Philip meant when he said, "If thou believest with all thine heart, thou mayest [be baptized]." If I have chosen the right word, then faith must be like all these other states of preparation. It is—for the believer in Christ is trimmed, trained, interested, desirous, loving and generated, for "he that believeth that Jesus is the Christ is begotten of God."

Passing from the column of preparation, we come to that of "CONSUMMATION." Here it will be seen that each of these states of preparation comes to some specific act, where it is consummated and finds its value. Trimming is consummated in grafting, interest in enlistment, desire in the oath of allegiance, love in the marriage ceremony and generation in birth. This teaches us that faith must come to some specific act, where it is consummated and finds its value. This action I have designated by the word "baptism." If I have chosen the right word, then baptism must be like all these other consummating acts. It is—for baptism is a grafting, an entry, an enlistment, an oath, a ceremony, a birth, for "except a man be born of water and the Spirit, he can not enter the kingdom of God."

From the column of consummation we pass to that of "PRODUCTS." Here you will note that each of these consummating acts brings forth a certain product. 1. Grafting produces a "branch." 2. Entry produces a "runner." 3. Enlistment produces a "soldier." 4. Oath produces a "citizen." 5. Ceremony produces a "bride." 6. Birth produces a "child." This teaches us that baptism, the consummating act of faith, must bring forth a certain product. This product I have designated in the diagram by the word "CHRISTIAN." If I have chosen the right word, then a Christian must be like all these other products. He is—for a Christian is a branch, a runner, a soldier, a citizen, a bride and a child, for "the Spirit itself beareth witness with our spirit that we are children of God." We hear much loose talk about "unbaptized Christians." I affirm in the light of these inspired illustrations that a citizen who had never taken the oath, a bride who had never been married, or a child who had never been born, would be an exact analogy to the Christian (?) who had never been baptized.

Leaving the column of products, we come to that of "BLESSINGS." Here you will notice that each of these products has a blessing in promise or possession. 1. The branch has "fruit." 2. The runner has "a crown." 3. The soldier has "a victory." 4. The citizen has "privileges." 5. The bride has "companionship." 6. The child has an "heirship." This teaches us that the Christian must have some blessing or blessings in promise or possession.

I have designated this blessing in the diagram by the word "SALVATION." If I have chosen the right word, then salvation must be like all these other blessings. It is—for the saved man bears fruit, wears a crown, achieves victories, enjoys privileges, has the company of Jesus, and is an heir, for "if children, then heirs—heirs of God and joint heirs with the Lord Jesus Christ."

The inevitable conclusion, then, from this diagram, based on the teachings of Christ and his apostles, is: 1. That Christ established a relation between man and God called the church. 2. That to be prepared for this relation, men must have a whole-hearted faith in Christ. 3. That to enter this relation men must be baptized. 4. That the baptized man is a Christian. 5. That the Christian enjoys salvation.

	RELATION.	PREPARATION.	CONSUMMATION.	PRODUCTION.	BLESSINGS.
John xv. 5.	Vine.	Trimming.	Grafting.	Branch.	Fruit.
Heb. xii. 1.	Race.	Training.	Entry.	Runner.	Grown.
II. Tim. ii. 4.	Army.	Interest.	Enlistment.	Soldier.	Victory.
Matt. xvi. 8.	CHURCH	FAITH	BAPTISM	CHRISTIAN	SALVATION
Eph. ii. 19.	Government.	Desire.	Oath.	Citizen.	Privilege.
Rom. vii. 4.	Matrimony.	Love.	Ceremony.	Bride.	Companionship.
Rom. viii. 16.	Family.	Generation.	Birth.	Child.	Heirship.

GRANVILLE JONES, Galveston, Tex.

II.—THE TWO COVENANTS.

REFERENCES:
$\begin{cases}\end{cases}$
Ex. xxxiv. 27, 28.
Deut. ix. 9–11.
I. Kings viii. 9–21.
Jer. xxxi. 31–34.
Matt. v. 17, 18 with John xix. 28–30.
II. Cor. iii. 3–11.
Gal. iii. 15–29.
Col. ii. 11–17.
Heb. viii.–x.

BETWEEN the promise made to Abraham (Gen. xii. 2, 3 ; xvii. 6-8) and the fulfillment in Christ (Acts iii. 24-26), came the *law* as a temporary dispensation for the Jews (Gal. iii. 16-19). This Mosaic dispensation is known as a *covenant*. Being a covenant with the Jews only, it was to be superceded by a " great salvation," which is for all people. Accordingly, " when the fullness of time was come, God sent forth his Son," who was the fulfillment of all that went before. The Epistle to the Hebrews is chiefly an explanation of the relation between the covenant through Moses and the one through Christ. The chart puts this relation before the eye. Reference to II. Cor. iii. 3-11, along with the letter to the Hebrews, especially the 8th, 9th and 10th chapters, teaches us the temporary nature of the one and the permanent nature of the other. On the left of the chart are the characteristics of the Old ; on the right those of the New Covenant, as they are called in Heb. viii. 13. Other items of contrast could be found for both the upper and lower part of the chart, *e. g.*, " By the Prophets," *vs.* " By His Son ; " " Words spoken by angels," *vs.* " The Great Salvation " (Heb. i. 1, 2 ; ii. 2, 3). The lower part of the chart sets forth the *loss* in abandoning the old covenant and the *gain* in receiving the new.

The Scriptures in Ex. xxxiv. 27, 28, Deut. ix. 9-11, and I. Kings viii. 9-21 prove the Ten Commandments to be at least a part of the old covenant which was " done away " in Christ. The cross marks the end of the old order (John xix. 28-30 ; Col. ii. 14) and the beginning of the new (Heb. ix. 16, 17). " Now the God of peace, that brought again from the dead our Lord Jesus, that great Shepherd of the sheep, through the blood *of the everlasting covenant*, make you perfect in every good work to do his will, working in you that which is well pleasing in his sight, through Jesus Christ ; to whom be glory for ever and ever. Amen."

THE TWO COVENANTS

OLD.

LAW "LETTER".

"Ministration of death"
"Tables of stone."
"That which is done away"

FIRST COVENANT.

LOSS.

1 Animal Sacrifice.
2 Fleshly Circumcision
3 Divers Washings.
4 Anointing with oil.
5 Passover Feast.
6 The Sabbath Day.

IT IS FINISHED

NEW.

GOSPEL "SPIRIT".

"Ministration of Righteousness." "Life"
"Fleshly tables of the heart."
"That which remaineth."

SECOND COVENANT.

GAIN.

1 A living interceeding Savior.
2 Circumcision of the heart.
3 Christian Baptism.
4 The Holy Spirit.
5 Communion or Lord's Supper.
6 The first day—Lord's Day.

W. W. SNIFF.

III.—Chart of Redemption, or Symbols of Salvation.

THE burden of preaching is to explain the salvation of the gospel, which is contained in figurative language. A map showing a full presentation of the figures of speech and their relation to each other, adds unity, clearness and fullness to the view. The too exclusive use of a single figure narrows, hardens and darkens the understanding.

Another difficulty overcome by this diagram is in preserving the words for the different conditions of lost, recovered and saved, etc., in unity with the proper word for the Saviour. The object of this chart, therefore, is:

1st. To show that our lost condition is represented under a variety of figures that have their base in our infirmities and misfortunes, as being sick, lost, slaves, ignorant, orphans, etc. Sixteen words are here given.

2nd. To show that our Saviour wears a name that corresponds in function to each one of these conditions. That is, to the "sick" he is the great "Physician;" to the "astray" he is the "Good Shepherd;" to the "slave" he is a great "Redeemer," a Father, etc. Sixteen are here given.

3rd. It shows sixteen words for convert, or words taken with their correlates that stand in the same relation to the change so called.

Thus the sick have a Physician who *heals* them; the lost are *found* by the Shepherd; the orphan is *adopted* by the Father, etc., etc.

4th. It shows sixteen words for the saved condition, as saints, guests, disciples, the just, etc., and it presents these on a line where the eye can follow each to its own symbolic relations, thus showing the fullness of the salvation offered to all conditions. Thus, if we were criminals, the Judge justified us (in Christ), and we are now the *just*. We were unclean, but God, the holy One, has sanctified us and made us *saints*. We were ignorant; he is the Teacher and taught us, and we became *disciples*, etc., etc.

5th. The diagram also illustrates that while there is redemption only in Christ, yet our condition is viewed from different states of alienation from God, and that we accept salvation from that point of departure, and that he has provided to save us wherein we needed saving; as the prisoner needs a pardon, the slave to be purchased, the sick a physician, the ignorant a teacher; and that to these the Saviour comes in the office that corresponds to their needs, respectively, and by his own blood pardons, purchases, heals, teaches, etc., and so saves and recovers.

6th. It will be observed that some of the words standing in the circle of convert are active and some are passive, and that these correspond to that functional name of the Saviour on the same line. Thus, as Creator he created us anew, but as Host he invited or called us, and we are as guests, etc.

Other analogies and suggestions can be illustrated from the diagram, as, for instance, it is wrong usage to use any word for convert more exclusive than the facts warrant, and the error of trying to make all individual conversions correspond to some one personal experience or standard, usually the teacher's own. It shows that the full preaching of the gospel must find its way to the variety of conditions in which men are lost, and that while Christ is the Saviour of all, conversions vary as do the conditions of the unsaved.

It also corrects the wrong usage of correlated symbols. It is wrong to say Christ teaches the unclean (he washes him), or that he cleanses the ignorant (he teaches him), or that he saved a slave (he purchased him), or that he healed a prisoner (he liberated him), etc., etc. The symbols for our alienated state are contained in the outer circle. The words that relate to our rescue are in the middle circle. The words in the inner circle are of the saved, wherein we have an Advocate with the Father, etc.

At the four quarters of the map are spiritual attributes of God: Love, Light, Spirit and Judgment.

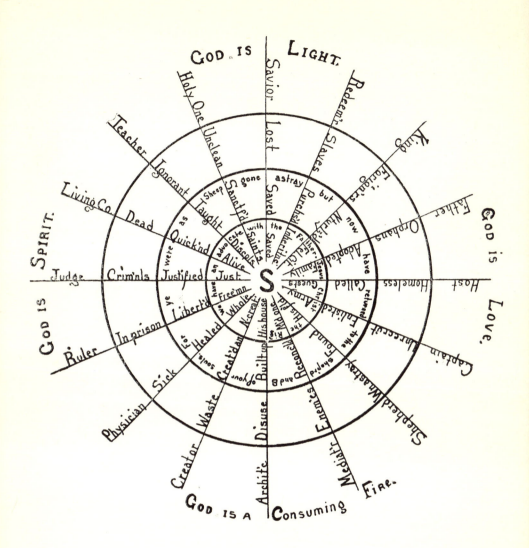

CHART OF REDEMPTION.

J. S. HUGHES, Englewood, Ill.

IV.—THE PROCESS OF CONVERSION.

IN this diagram eight representative cases of conversion, recorded in the Book of Acts, are chosen for the purpose of exhibiting the steps in the process.

These eight cases include all in which there is any attempt at detailed description.

The diagram as a whole shows the steps to be: (1) Hearing; (2) Faith ; (3) Repentance ; (4) Confession ; (5) Baptism.

Each column presents a particular case and shows the steps which are specifically mentioned and those which are left to be inferred.

The Authorized Version is followed in this study.

A distinction is made between *necessary inference* and *fair inference ; e. g.*, Repentance is mentioned in connection with two cases only, but as repentance involves a change of mind as well as reformation of life, it is inconceivable that the latter steps would have been taken without this. The same reasoning applies to faith. Confession, however, is only fairly inferred, because it is conceivable that a peni- tent believer might have been admitted to baptism without the formal confession with the mouth. Yet, because of the fact that emphasis is laid upon this in other places in the New Testament, notably in Rom. x. 9, 10, we may *fairly infer* that it was not omitted in these cases.

It will be noticed that the emphasis of *special mention* is greatest upon the *first* and *last* steps—the first, *hearing*, being mentioned in six out of eight cases, and the *last*, baptism, being mentioned in *every* case.

THE PROCESS OF CONVERSION, AS SHOWN BY REPRESENTATIVE CASES IN ACTS.

STEPS IN PROCESS.	Acts ii. PENTECOST.	Acts viii. SAMARITANS.	Acts viii. THE EUNUCH.	Acts ix. SAUL.	Acts x. CORNELIUS.	Acts xvi. LYDIA.	Acts xvi. THE JAILOR.	Acts xviii. CORINTHIANS.
HEARING.	S. M. Ver. 37.	S. M. Ver. 6.	N. I.	S. M. Ver. 4.	S. M. Ver 33.	S. M. Ver. 14.	N. I.	S. M. Ver. 8
FAITH.	N. I.	S. M. Ver. 12.	S. M. Ver. 37.	S. M. Ver. 38.	S. M. Ver. 43.	N. I.	S. M. Vers. 31-34.	S. M. Ver. 8.
REPENTANCE.	S. M. Ver. 38.	N. I.	N. I.	N. I.	S. M. Ch. xi. 18.	N. I.	N. I.	N. I.
CONFESSION.	F. I.	F. I.	S. M. Ver. 37.	F. I.	F. I.	F. I.	F. I.	F. I.
BAPTISM.	S. M. Vers. 38-41.	S. M. Ver. 12.	S. M. Ver. 38.	S. M. Ver. 18.	S. M. Vers. 47, 48.	S. M. Ver. 15.	S. M. Ver. 33.	S. M. Ver. 8.

☞ In the above, S. M. means *special mention*; N. I., *necessary inference*; F. I., *fair inference.*

GEO. A. LORD, Painesville, O.

V.—"THE SOLID ROCK."

PART I.—THE ARCH.

WE here build the principal elements of the story of Jesus into an arch. Do we believe that Jesus is divine because the Bible teaches it? or do we believe the Bible is inspired because it contains the story of Jesus, and he endorses that book? Both are true, and these propositions support each other. Now note some principles in the construction of an arch:

(1) It must have a solid foundation.

(2) The blocks in the arch must have a like solidity—not part granite and part pasteboard.

(3) Either there must be a key-stone at the center of the arch, or each block must contain the key-stone principle.

(4) When properly built an arch is made stronger by weights upon it until ground to powder.

The Christ-story as an arch forming the Rock of Ages:

The *foundation* consists of the Incarnation on the one hand and the Resurrection and Ascension of Jesus on the other. These are partly out of our sight—we can not fully comprehend them—but we know that a foundation that can sustain such an arch as we see here must be solid *granite* and not *pasteboard*. The *blocks* in the arch are all named and can be described and explained in full to a congregation.

PART II.

We now have the arch on which we are to build our hopes of eternal life. Will the woes and sorrows of earth break it down? We shall see.

(1) When our earthly hope deferred makes the heart sick, if our expectation is from the Lord, we shall not be disappointed.

(2) As we can carry no worldly goods away with us, it matters little if we only have a good foundation for the future, and that is on this Rock.

(3) False friends will forsake us in trouble, but the Lord will not.

(4) Men may prove untrue, but Christ can not deny himself.

(5) God does not tempt us, but will rescue us from Satan.

(6) If we are poor in worldly goods, we may be rich toward God.

(7) When the rich oppress the poor, their hope is in the Lord of Hosts who hears their cry.

(8) Sickness without Christ is loss; with him it is gain.

(9) A precipice is before a position without God; but his children in high places are a blessing to the world. See Garfield, Gladstone and Victoria.

(10) A weak man is ruined by "good society;" but a strong and brave Christian brings his associates into the kingdom with him.

(11) An office is dangerous to a man whose life is not consecrated to Christ; but a true man will use it to honor the name of his Master.

(12) Riches are a heavy weight on the arch, but if sanctified become most useful.

(13) Business may be made to choke out the Word of God, or to honor his name—just as we use it.

(14) Money is always scarce when we are without it; our policy-seeking friends depart with our substance; but the Lord will stay.

(15) We can honor God in any honorable profession.

(16) Sudden poverty only drives the good man to God.

(17) In death there is no book like the Bible and no friend like Jesus.

(18) There are neither running sands nor swinging pendulums with the kingdom of God. Earthly things must pass away, but it will stand forever.

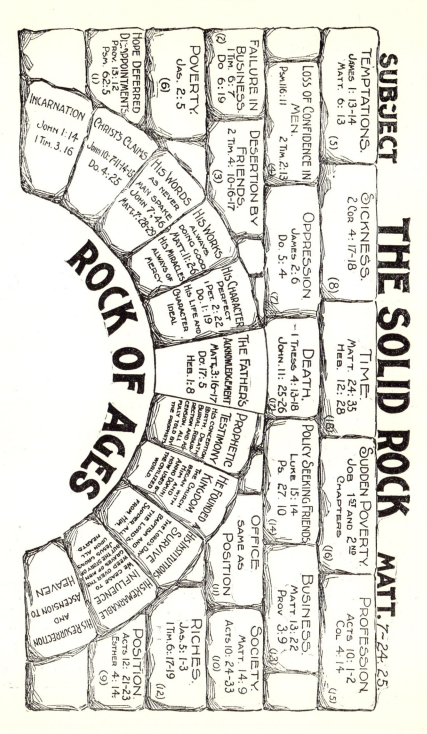

THE SOLID ROCK

MATT. 7:24-25.

SUBJECT

TEMPTATIONS.
JAMES 1: 13-14
MATT. 6: 13
(5)

LOSS OF CONFIDENCE IN MEN.
PSM 116: 11
2 TIM. 2:13
(4)

FAILURE IN BUSINESS.
1 TIM. 6:7
DO 6:19
(2)

POVERTY.
JAS. 2:5
(6)

HOPE DEFERRED
DISAPPOINTMENTS.
PROV. 13:12
PSM. 62:5
(1)

SICKNESS.
2 COR 4: 17-18

OPPRESSION.
JAMES 2:6
DO 5: 4
(7)

DESERTION BY FRIENDS.
2 TIM. 4: 10-16-17
(3)

INCARNATION
JOHN 1: 14
1 TIM. 3. 16

CHRIST'S CLAIMS
JOHN 10: 7-11-14-15
DO. 4: 25

HIS WORDS
AS NEVER MAN SPAKE
JOHN 7: 46
MATT. 7: 28-29

HIS WORKS
ALWAYS DOING GOOD
MATT. 11: 2-5
HIS MIRACLES ALWAYS OF MERCY.

HIS CHARACTER
PERFECT
1 PET. 2: 22
DO. 1: 19
HIS LIFE AND CHARACTER IDEAL

TIME.
MATT. 24:35
HEB. 12: 28

DEATH.
1 THESS 4:13-18
JOHN 11: 25-26
(17)

THE FATHER'S PROPHETIC TESTIMONY
ACKNOWLEDGMENT
MATT.3:16-17
DO. 17: 5
HEB. 1: 8

HE FOUNDED A KINGDOM

HIS INSTITUTIONS

BAPTISM AND THE LORD'S DAY.

HIS PROPHETIC HISTORY
HIS CONCEPTION, BIRTH, DEATH, BURIAL, RESURRECTION AND ASCENSION. ALL FULLY TOLD BY THE PROPHET.

SUDDEN POVERTY.
JOB 1ST AND 2ND CHAPTERS
(18)

POLICY SEEKING FRIENDS.
LUKE 15:14
PS. 27: 10
(14)

OFFICE
SAME AS POSITION
(11)

BUSINESS.
MATT. 13:22
PROV. 3:9
(13)

PROFESSION.
ACTS 10: 1-2
COL 4: 14
(15)

SOCIETY.
MATT. 14:9
ACTS 10: 24-33
(10)

RICHES.
JAS 5: 1-3
1 TIM. 6: 17-19
(12)

POSITION.
ACTS 12: 21-23
ESTHER 4: 14.
(9)

SURVIVE.

HIS REMARKABLE INFLUENCE
THE LORD'S SUPPER. ALL JESUS GLORY, BUT STORY OF GRAVES OR MEN. WE CEASE TO WEEP OVER THE GRAVES OF MEN, UPON ALL HEARTS. FROM HIM.

HIS RESURRECTION AND ASCENSION TO HEAVEN.

ROCK OF AGES

VI.—THE FALL AND RESTORATION OF MAN.

MAN was created in the likeness and image of God. He was placed in the garden to dress and keep it. He lost this glorious and beautiful home. How? Reflect. Did he "fall"? Strictly speaking, he did not. Rather he came down step by step. He was not overpowered, he was not forced; but, by exercising his God-given faculties, he followed his own desires, and voluntarily abandoned his beautiful home and surrendered his claims to purity and innocency. Let us follow him. Note: (1) He was approached by the tempter. (2) The tempter spoke to him—to his affections, mind, conscience and destiny. (3) He believed, and his belief was based upon the testimony that had been adduced. (4) He turned away from God. (5) He turned toward Satan. (6) He broke the positive, Divine law when he touched and ate of the forbidden tree. (7) Guilt followed transgression, immediately and inevitably. (8) Expulsion from the garden. (9) A state of sin and condemnation and death. (10) Everlasting destruction. Note, also, that there were three changes wrought: (1) A change of heart or affections. (2) A change of mind or thought. (3) A change of state or relationship. Contemplate man "in the world," in sin. His relations to God and the universe have been changed, alas! How radical the change. Yet he has not lost all. He is still a man. He is still made in the likeness and image of God. He still has a memory. He still has a will power. He still possesses reason. He is depraved, but not totally depraved. Contrast this state with his Edenic home. Contrast thorns and thistles with flowers that ever bloom, and beauties that never fade.

Contemplate man as he is being restored to God. Force plays no part. Persuasion is everything. Let us follow him. Note: (1) Study the life and character of the Redeemer who comes into the world to save sinners (I. Tim. i. 15). Contrast his mission with the mission of Satan. (2) The Redeemer speaks, entreats, commands. (3) Man must believe (John xx. 30, 31). (4) He must turn to God (Mal. iii. 7; Acts xxvi. 18). (5) He must turn from Satan (Jas. iv. 7, 8). (6) He must submit to the positive divine law in baptism (Mark xvi. 15, 16; Acts ii. 38; Rom. vi. 1-5, 16-18; Gal. iii. 25-27). (7) Remission of sins, justification, sanctification, gift of the Holy Spirit (Acts ii. 38; iii. 32). (8) Admission into the Church of God in Christ (Acts ii. 47). (9) A state of sobriety, righteousness and godliness (Tit. ii. 11-14). (10) Everlasting life. Note also that three changes are wrought: (1) A change of affection. He no longer loves sin. He loves God supremely. (2) A change of mind or thought. (3) A change of state or relationship. The Christian enjoys new relations—to God, to man, to the universe. How comprehensive, how radical the change! But he is still a man. Temptations lie before him. "Much land remains to be conquered." The grave and the "unseen world" lie beyond him. How changed his tastes, desires and aspirations. Contrast his state with his former condition. Exhort to steadfastness and to purity.

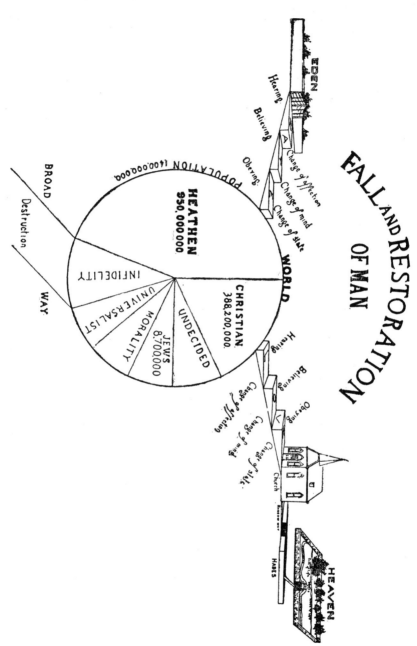

FALL AND RESTORATION OF MAN

POPULATION 1,400,000,000

HEATHEN 950,000,000

CHRISTIAN 388,200,000

JEWS 8,700,000

INFIDELITY

UNIVERSALIST

MORALITY

UNDECIDED

BROAD

Destruction

WAY

WORLD

EDEN

Hearing
Believing
Obeying
Change of affection
Change of mind
Change of state

Hearing
Believing
Obeying
Change of affection
Change of mind
Change of state

Church

HADES

HEAVEN

ASHLEY S. JOHNSON, LL. D.
School of the Evangelists, Kimberlin Heights, Tenn.

VII.—THE GOLDEN CHAIN.

THE diagram is an illustration of salvation by grace through faith. There are two sides to salvation—the human and the divine. Faith is the human side, or man's part, and grace, the divine side, or God's part.

Definitions: Grace—favor—a gift. Faith, in its fullness, submission and service. Grace, then, is what God has given to procure man's salvation, and faith is what man must do to appropriate it. The diagram puts it in concrete, tangible form. The eye can behold it.

Taking it up in order, we have:

1. The circle, the symbol of perfection, which is God.

2. The Saviour, the first element of God's grace—his best gift. The brace to the right encloses what were necessary to constitute him a Saviour.

3. The Spirit, the second element of God's grace. His threefold office work is indicated to the right.

4. The Scriptures, the third element of God's grace. These three gifts—Saviour, Spirit, Scriptures—constitute God's grace in the concrete. They are the embodiment, the manifestations of his grace.

Beginning at the bottom, we have:

1. The sinner in the condition described. His eternal salvation depends upon his being linked in eternal union with God. It takes just two links to effect this union, viz.: Submission and service. This submission is a complete surrender to Christ. *To the thoroughly enlightened* man's submission, the elements indicated to the right are essential—all of them. Will not God's mercy supply the lack of others? (See Rom. ii. 25–29.)

2. Service, such as is here described, perpetuates the union between God and man, in which is everlasting life—eternal salvation.

THE GOLDEN CHAIN

EPH. 2:7-9

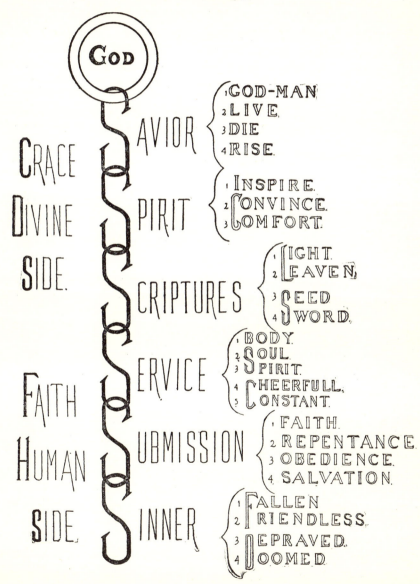

GOD

GRACE
DIVINE
SIDE.

FAITH
HUMAN
SIDE.

SAVIOR
1 GOD-MAN
2 LIVE
3 DIE
4 RISE.

SPIRIT
1 INSPIRE.
2 CONVINCE.
3 COMFORT.

SCRIPTURES
1 LIGHT.
2 LEAVEN.
3 SEED
4 SWORD.

SERVICE
1 BODY.
2 SOUL.
3 SPIRIT.
4 CHEERFULL.
5 CONSTANT.

SUBMISSION
1 FAITH.
2 REPENTANCE.
3 OBEDIENCE.
4 SALVATION.

SINNER
1 FALLEN
2 FRIENDLESS.
3 DEPRAVED.
4 DOOMED.

W. H. BAGBY.

VIII.—NEW TESTAMENT BAPTISMS.

TEXT—Matt. iii. 11.

THERE are three baptisms mentioned in this verse, but none of them are Christian baptism. There are four in the New Testament, including that.

(1) John's baptism was designed to prepare the Jews to receive Christ, and they that would not come "rejected the counsel of God against themselves," and did not believe in him when he came.

(2) The baptism of the Holy Spirit was designed to qualify the apostles for the special work of spreading the gospel to the ends of the earth, and refers to the twelve from the fact that the pronoun "they" in Acts ii. (1, 2, 3, 4 verses) has for its antecedent Matthias and the Eleven of Acts i. 26, and not the 120 of Acts i. 15, as some suppose. Only three cases of Holy Spirit baptism in the New Testament. Read Acts ii. 1-4, Acts x. 44-41 and Acts xi. 15; also xix. 6. One peculiarity of Holy Ghost baptism is, they always spoke with "tongues," or in unknown languages, a thing that does not happen since the days of miracles are past.

(3) Christian baptism is the ceremony whereby we are brought into relationship with Christ—separated from the world; dead to sin; buried with Christ; and now have access to his grace, wherein we stand.

(4) Baptism of fire means immersed in fire. Read Rev. xx. 10-15 and xix. 20. This refers to the final judgment—the doom of those who reject the gospel.

New Testament Baptism.

1. { Baptism of John. — A Command — Before the Cross.
   - John --------------- The Administrator.
   - Water --------------- The Element.
   - Believing Jews --------------- The Subjects.
   - Prepare for Christ --------------- The Design.

2. { Baptism of Holy Spirit. — A Promise — At Pentecost.
   - Christ --------------- The Administrator.
   - Holy Spirit --------------- The Element.
   - Apostles --------------- The Subject.
   - Qualify them (special work) --------------- The Design.

3. { Baptism of Commission. — **Command to Believers.**
   - Gospel Preacher --------------- The Administrator.—Matt. xxviii. 19.
   - Water --------------- The Element.—Acts viii. 36.
   - Penitent Believer --------------- The Subject.—Acts viii. 36.
   - Remission of Past Sins --------------- The Design.—Acts ii. 38.

4. { Baptism of Fire. — A Threat — At Judgment.
   - Christ --------------- The Administrator.
   - Fire --------------- The Element.
   - Unbelievers --------------- The Subject.
   - Punishment --------------- The Design.

IX.—WHAT IS THE GOSPEL?

TEXT—Rom. xv. 29.

THE word "gospel" means "good provided." The idea expanded into "the Gospel" signifies the *means* prepared for our salvation.

"The Gospel" contains "fullness of blessing" (Rom. xv. 29). It brings "*joy* to all people" (Luke ii. 10). It is an expression of "grace" (Acts xx. 24). It embraces *three* fundamental *facts* as the foundation stones of *belief* (I. Cor. xv. 1–5). The Gospel can not be "obeyed" (Rom. x. 16) without *commands* (Acts xvi. 31; ii. 38). Neither is there a well-grounded "hope of the Gospel" without *promises* (Col. i. 23; Acts ii. 38; I. Pet. i. 3, 4).

And the Master hand now adds the glories of the Gospel (II. Cor. iv. 4). It is "glorious" because it *expresses* God, as the splendid steam-engine expresses the mind of its maker. It will exclude and eclipse all, as the sun puts out the light of the moon and chases away the stars by its own glory and effulgence.

Lastly, the Gospel is glorious because it effects God's great purpose—*salvation.*

Illustrate this last point by cases of "Blue Dick," "Life of Knowles Shaw."

GOSPEL

"GOOD NEWS."

1. "BLESSING."   —   *Rom. xv.* 29.

2. "JOY."   —   —   *Luke ii.* 10.

3. "GRACE."   —   —   *Acts xx.* 24.

4. FACTS.
{ Death.
  Burial.
  Resurrection. }   *I. Cor xv.* 1–5.

5. COMMANDS.
{ Believe.
  Repent.
  Be Baptized. }   *Rom. x.* 16.

6. PROMISES.
{ Remission.
  Gift of H. S.
  Eternal Life. }   *Col. i.* 23.

7. GLORIES.
{ Expresses God.
  Eclipses All.
  Effects Purpose. }   *II. Cor. iv.* 4.

J. H. PAINTER.

X.—THE GOSPEL.

OSPEL means the good news, and is in the New Testament the news of salvation through Christ. It is placed in the center because it is the center of all God's plans for the human race.

II. The Gospel has its purposes and its agencies. The purposes are two, viz: 1. To save man from sin. 2. To fit him for glory. It likewise has two agencies, viz: 1. Divine. 2. Human.

III. The divine agents are: 1. The Father, who (a) by wisdom plans; (b) by power executes, and (c) by love tenders salvation to man. 2. The Son, who (a) by his life sets an example; (b) by his death offers a propitiation for our sin; (c) by his resurrection gives a pledge of eternal life to man. 3. The Holy Spirit, who (a) confirms the apostles' doctrine by "signs, wonders and divers miracles;" (b) glorifies Christ through the preaching of the apostles; (c) comforts the Christian.

IV. The human agents are: 1. The apostles, who (a) testify to what they have seen, and can therefore have no successors; (b) proclaim salvation in the name of Jesus Christ upon the terms of the gospel; (c) exhort men to save themselves by accepting the free tender of salvation. 2. The Church, which (a) maintains the ordinances, baptism being the privilege of the alien, and is performed but once, and at entrance into Christ; the Lord's Supper being the privilege of the child, and is performed weekly in imitation of apostolic example; (b) holds forth the Word of Life. It is called the Word of Life because it reveals life, imparts life, governs life; (c) invites sinners to salvation. "The Spirit and the bride say, Come." 3. The world—by which is meant that part of humanity that is without God and "without hope in the world"—which (a) believes the gospel upon the testimony of the truth; (b) reforms, by repenting of sin, confessing Christ and obeying the gospel command of baptism; (c) receives the promise of remission of sins, the gift of the Holy Spirit, priestly intercession, fatherly guidance, the communion of the saints and the life everlasting.

V. The upper and outer hemicircle embraces all that is contained in heaven's offer of salvation. The lower embraces all that is contained in man's acceptance of it.

FAITH.

FAITH, CONVICTION AND CONFIDENCE. (Heb. xi. 1.)

I. Faith (Acts vi. 7; Gal. i. 23) comes by preaching.

1. WHEN?
- (a) AFTER CHRIST'S RESURRECTION.
- (b) AT BEGINNING. Luke xxiv. 47; Acts xi. 15.
- (c) PENTECOST. Acts ii.

2. WHERE?
- (a) IN JERUSALEM.
- (b) IN JUDÆA.
- (c) IN SAMARIA.
- (d) EVERYWHERE. Acts i. 8.

3. HOW?
- (a) BY REVELATION. Gal. i. 12.
- (b) BY PREACHING. I. Cor. i. 21.
- (c) BY WRITING. Epistles.

4. WHY?
- (a) TO GIVE LIGHT. Acts xxvi. 18.
- (b) TO CORRECT ERROR. II. Tim. iii. 16, 17.
- (c) TO SAVE BELIEVERS. Rom. i. 16.

II. Confidence comes by hearing. (Rom. x. 17.)

1. WHEN?
- (a) AFTER PREACHING. Rom. x. 14.
- (b) AFTER HEARING. Eph. i. 13.
- (c) AFTER UNDERSTANDING. Matt. xiii. 23.
- (d) IN OBEDIENCE. Rom. x. 16; Jas. ii. 26.

2. WHERE?
- (a) IN THE HEART. Rom. x. 9.
- (b) IN THE MOUTH. Rom.
- (c) IN THE LIFE. Jas. ii. 18.

3. HOW?
- (a) WITH THE HEART. Rom. x. 10.
- (b) WITH THE UNDERSTANDING. Eph. i. 18.
- (c) BY OBEDIENCE. Jas. ii. 18.

4. WHY?
- (a) TO UNDERSTAND. Ps. xix. 11.
- (b) TO HAVE THE SPIRIT. Gal. iii. 2-5.
- (c) TO ESCAPE CONDEMNATION. Mark xvi. 16.
- (d) TO PLEASE GOD. Heb. xi. 6.

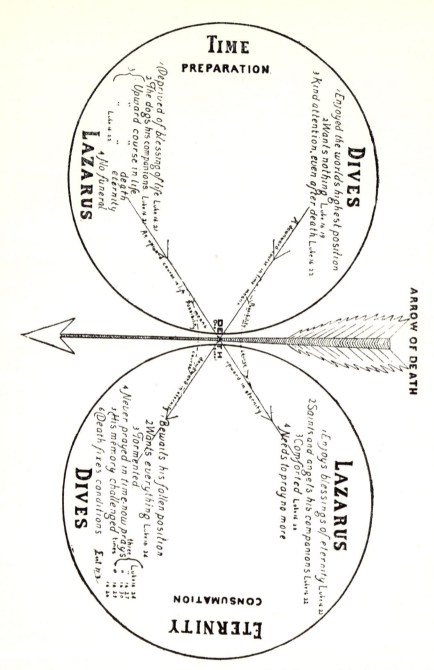

XIII.—THE TABERNACLE.

TO GET before our readers a clear and satisfactory idea of the Tabernacle, we must describe 1. Its structure. 2. Its furniture. 3. Its service. 4. Its typical import.

I. STRUCTURE OF THE TABERNACLE.

The entire Tabernacle court was 50 cubits, or 75 feet wide, north and south, and 150 feet long, east and west. This space was covered by curious screens, in the East called *kannauts*, and still used to enclose the private apartments of important personages. They were 7½ feet high, and supported by pillars of brass or bronze 7½ feet apart, to which the curtains were attached by hooks and fillets of silver (Ex. xxvii. 9, etc.). At the east end, however—the end of entrance—it was closed by curtains of fine twined linen, wrought with needle-work, and of the most gorgeous colors. This entrance was 30 feet wide.

The Tent was placed within the enclosure, in the western half, facing toward the east. It was 45 feet long, and 15 feet broad. If, however, as is most probable, the roof was pitched like a roof of a house, the two sides overhung the wall on either side 7½ feet, so that the entire width of the Tabernacle was about 30 feet. The gables of the roof were east and west. The walls north, south and west were formed of boards of shittim wood—supposed to be the acacia, the most durable wood known in the peninsula—15 feet high, covered with gold, while at the eastern end, or entrance, there was a veil adorned with needle work, hung by golden hooks to five pillars of gold-covered acacia, resting on bases of bronze. The boards had two tenons at the lower end, which fitted into silver bases, and at the top they were joined and fastened together by bars of acacia wood, run through rings of gold (Ex. xxvi. 15 29). The roof was formed by four sets of curtains—the innermost of fine twined linen, of various colors, and ornamented (Ex. xxvi. 1, etc.); the next of goats' hair cloth (xxvi. 7); the next of rams' skins, dyed red (xxvi. 14); and the next of badgers' skins, or more probably seal skins (xxv. 5). It is generally supposed these last were a mere coping or ridge-piece. For the minuter details concerning these coverings, we refer to the descriptions in Exodus, and the comments in Smith's Bible Dictionary and the Bible Commentary.

This tent or tabernacle was divided into two apartments—the western being 15 feet square, and the eastern 15 by 30 feet. The western or innermost apartment was called the Holy of Holies, or Holiest of all; the other was called simply the Holy Place. The partition was formed by a curtain or veil, made of richest material, adorned with cherubs, and hung by golden hooks to four pillars of acacia covered with gold.

We have, then, altogether, three divisions within the enclosure. Entering at the east end, we have 1. The outer court, embracing one-half of the entire area. 2. The Holy Place of the Tabernacle, 15 by 30 feet. 3. The Holy of Holies, 15 feet square. A rough sketch of these divisions is here given. Let it be observed that the two rooms in the Tabernacle *receive no light from without;* they have no windows, and no means of admitting light from without, unless the curtain at the east end is raised for that purpose.

II. THE FURNITURE.

1. *The Furniture of the Outer Court.*—Entering from the east end of the enclosure, we come, first, to the *altar of burnt offerings,* where the sacrifices were offered (Ex. xl. 6); and then, between that and the entrance to the Holy Place, to the *laver*—a brass or copper vessel, containing water, at which the priests were to wash before going into the Holy Place (Ex. xl. 7; xxx. 18-21).

2. *The Furniture of the Holy Place.*—Entering from the outer court at the east end of the Holy Place, at your right, or on the north side, will be seen *the table of shew bread,* on which twelve loaves are placed—the loaves being renewed every sabbath. On it are also found dishes, cups or saucers, and bowls or *wine-cups,* for although no wine-drinking or libations are mentioned in connection with this part of the service, the bowls or wine-cups are there, and the Jewish tradition is that a bowl of excellent wine was always kept upon the table, and that once a week, when the bread was changed, the contents were poured out as a libation before the Lord. (See Ex. xxv. 23-30.) On your left, on the south side, is a golden chandelier with seven branches, and a lamp supported on each. These are kept continually burning, fed with pure olive oil (Ex. xxvii. 20) to give light in this apartment, as it receives no light from without (Ex. xxv. 31-40). Looking toward the veil, the only other article of furniture seen in this room is *the altar of incense* (Ex. xxx. 1-10). This was also acacia, overlaid with pure gold. On this altar incense was regularly burned, morning and evening—fire being taken from the altar of burnt offerings for this purpose. (See Lev. x. 1, 2.) Here then, we have: 1. The table of bread and wine. 2. The golden candelabrum. 3. The altar of incense.

3. *The Furniture of the Holy of Holies.*—In this apartment there is but one article of furniture—*the Ark of the Testimony* (Ex. xxv. 10-22). This ark contains the tables of the law, a pot of manna, and Aaron's rod (Heb. ix. 4). It was covered by the mercy-seat, a lid of pure gold, which had at each

end a gold cherub; their faces are turned towards each other, and at the same time look down in ceaseless gaze upon the mercy-seat. Here, between the cherubs, over the ark of the covenant, and over the mercy-seat, dwells the *Shekinah*—the visible manifestation of Jehovah's presence; so that God himself is the light of this apartment. The Outer Court enjoys the light of Nature; the Holy Place is lighted by the seven golden lamps; the Holy of Holies is made light by God's own presence. Let the reader get these three divisions, with their furniture, fairly fixed in his mind.

III. THE SERVICE.

To understand this, we must have a distinct understanding of the *three divisions of persons* cor. responding to the three divisions of the sacred enclosure. 1. In the Outer Court, where the altar of sacrifice and the laver stood, *all the people* were allowed to come. 2. In the Holy Place, where were found the table of shew bread, the golden lampstand, and the altar of incense, *none but priests* could enter (Ex. xxx. 19-21, xl. 31, 32). 3. Into the Holy of Holies, where the ark of the covenant and the mercy-seat were, *none but the High Priest* could enter, and he only once a year, on the day of annual-atonement (Lev. xvi.).

In the Outer Court a burnt offering was consumed every morning and evening (Ex. xxix. 38-46). Here also God met with his people when they brought their sin-offerings, peace-offerings, and whatever the law required them to offer. (See Lev. i.—vii.) It was here forgiveness was assured to those who brought to the altar the sacrifices required by the law. Here, too, on the day of annual atonement, the nation, by its representatives, met and made the national offering, and obtained the pledge of pardon through the high priest (Lev. xvi.). Here, too, was the *laver* or *bath*, at which every priest was required to wash, before entering into the Holy Place (Ex. xxx. 18-21).

On going from the altar and the laver the priests entered the Holy Place. Here they placed on the table, every sabbath, new loaves of bread, and, we suppose, a fresh supply of wine; and here the priests ate the loaves, and poured out the wine, before the Lord (Ex. xxxvii. 10-16; Lev. xxiv. 5-9). Here they trimmed and fed the golden lamp daily (Ex. xxx. 7, 8; Lev. xxiv. 4). And here they burned incense twice a day upon the golden altar (Ex. xxx. 6-10). Here were food, light, and grateful worship, in which they "drew near" to God, coming close up to the veil, which alone separated them from the immediate presence of Jehovah.

Once a year the high priest went through the veil into the Holy of Holies, bearing on his shoulders and on his breast the names of the tribes of Israel, and bearing the blood of the victim slain for the sins of the people, which he sprinkled before the mercy-seat and upon the mercy-seat, while clouds of incense filled the place (Lev. xvi. 11-17). He went in dressed in the robes of an ordinary priest, but came forth arrayed in his magnificent robes, to bestow upon the people the pledge of pardon he had received from God (Ex. xxviii. 29, 30; Lev. xvi. 23, 24). Here, too, through Urim and Thummim (Ex. xxviii. 30) knowledge was obtained from the Lord and communicated to the people (Ex. xxv. 22).

Read also, in reference to the Tabernacle service, Heb. ix. 1-7.

IV. THE TYPICAL IMPORT OF THIS SERVICE.

We have not full information on this head, but we have sufficiently clear intimations to guide us to settled conclusions in many important particulars.

1. Paul assures us, respecting this whole service, that it was a *figure* or *parable* (*parabole*) in which one thing is put for another (Heb. ix. 9). He reasons, moreover, that since all things in the tabernacle service were made after patterns shown in the mount, they were "*patterns of heavenly things*," and that "the heavenly things themselves" are now revealed through Christ (Heb. ix. 23). The law had "a *shadow* of things to come" (Heb. x. 1; Col. ii. 16, 17).

2. The Jewish high priest was a type of Jesus, the High Priest of our confession (Heb. viii. 1-6); the sacrifices he offered, of the one great sacrifice for sin (Heb. x. 11, 12); and the Holy of Holies, a type of heaven itself into which our High Priest has entered with his own blood (Heb. ix. 24-28). Moses was the type of Christ as *mediator* (Heb. viii. 6; ix. 11-23).

3. The common priests were types of Christians, who are therefore described as "a holy priesthood, to offer up spiritual sacrifices" (I. Pet. ii. 5; Rev. i. 5, 6). And as the Holy of Holies, where the High Priest ministered, was typical of heaven itself, it is not difficult to conclude that the Holy Place where the ordinary priests ministered, was typical of the *Church* in which Christians minister.

What have we, then, in the Church, answering to the types in the Holy Place?

(1) Christians, a holy priesthood, to offer up spiritual sacrifices.

(2) The bread and wine on the Lord's table, renewed every Lord's day, to be appropriated by the priests. Not twelve loaves, for there are not twelve tribes of Israel; but "one loaf" and "one body." If any one thinks this is simply ingenious, and presses a more general interpretation of the type as simply indicating spiritual food and refreshment, we shall not pause to argue the question.

(3) The golden lamps giving light to this apartment, seem necessarily to typify the Spirit's revelations of truth and grace—that word which is "as a lamp shining in a dark place." "The entrance of thy word giveth light; it giveth understanding to the simple."

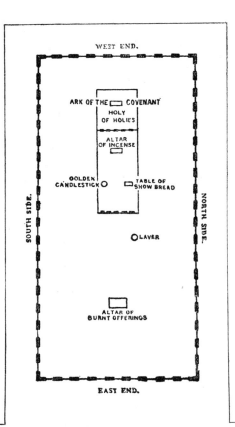

THREE DIVISIONS.

Type: 1. Outer Court. 2. Holy Place. 3. Holy of Holies.
Antitype: 1. The World. 2. The Church. 3. Heaven.

THREE CLASSES.

Type: 1. The People. 2. The Priests. 3. The High Priest.
Antitype: 1. Mankind. 2. Christians. 3. Jesus, our High Priest.

THREE SOURCES OF LIGHT.

Type: 1. The Sun. 2. The Seven Lamps. 3. The Glory of the Lord.
Antitype: 1. The Light of 2. The Perfect Light of 3. The Light of God's
Nature. God's Word. Presence.

THREE SOURCES OF BLESSING.

Type: 1. Altar, Laver. 2. Bread, Lamps, Incense. 3. The Shekinah.
Antitype: 1. Faith in Jesus 2. The Lord's Supper, the 3. The Divine Presence.
and Baptism. Word of God, Prayer
and Praise.

XIV.—"Chronological Diagram of Bible Periods and Events."

THE author offers an apology for this explanation, feeling that the diagram has upon its face quite as much as is herein stated. But, as suggestive, I submit the following :

ABBREVIATIONS.

DISPENSATION A.—ADAMIC DISPENSATION.
DISPENSATION M.—MOSAIC DISPENSATION.
DISPENSATION C.—CHRISTIAN DISPENSATION.
P.—PERIOD.   PS.—PERIODS.

When the numbers 1, 2, 3, etc., are used, we refer to the period or circle bearing that number in the dispensation under which we are speaking.

I now stand before you pointing to the diagram: Adam, Moses, Christ, Eden, Sinai, Zion. We start upon a journey "from Genesis to Revelation." Dispensation A. is divided into Periods 1 and 2 by the flood. P. 1 is from the beginning to the flood, and is divided into Ps. 3 and 4. P. 3 is from the beginning to the fall. P. 4 is from the fall to the close of P. 1, and contains P. 5—Noah, a preacher of righteousness. P. 2 is from the flood to the close of Dispensation A., and within it are Ps. 6 and 7. P. 6 is from the flood to the famine, and has Noah, his sons, tower of Babel, etc., as indicated in same. P. 7 is Israel in Egypt.

We now cross the *Red Sea* and enter Dispensation M. It has four leading periods. P. 1 is the forty years in the wilderness, and is from the Red Sea to the Jordan. P. 2, the children of Israel cross the Jordan, conquer the land, and are under Judges 355 years. They ask for a king. Saul is anointed, and thus we enter P. 3. It is from the first king to the "final captivity." The diagram in P. 3 indicates when the kingdom divided and other important events. P. 4 is next, which has Ps. 5, 6 and 7. P. 5 is very interesting, and is fully explained to the average Bible reader by the names within it. P. 6, from Malachi to John. is about 397 years of duration, concerning which the Bible tells us but little or nothing. P. 7 has a very full account compared with other Bible periods in duration ; Matthew, Mark, Luke, John, and two chapters of Acts being devoted to a period of only about thirty-three years. Pentecost has now come, and we enter the *Christian Dispensation*, which has two leading divisions. P. 1 is from "Pentecost" to the return of the Christ, at which time the "first resurrection" takes place, and we enter P. 2, which closes with the Judgment. P. 1 has Ps. 3 and 4, well understood by almost all Christian people, and which fully explain themselves.

One special merit which this diagram claims, is by the use of circles that it expresses a period or periods *within* another period, and that without the confusion of thought and appearance so often in diagrams. (See Ps. 3, 4 and 5, in P. 1 of Dispensation A.) This diagram was originally designed for a single lecture, but the author has found it very helpful in a series, taking, say, P. 1, for the first lecture, etc. He recently used it in a series of "fifteen minute" lectures in connection with the prayer-meeting, and the interest became so great that the house was filled. I find it a good starter and helper in Bible study.

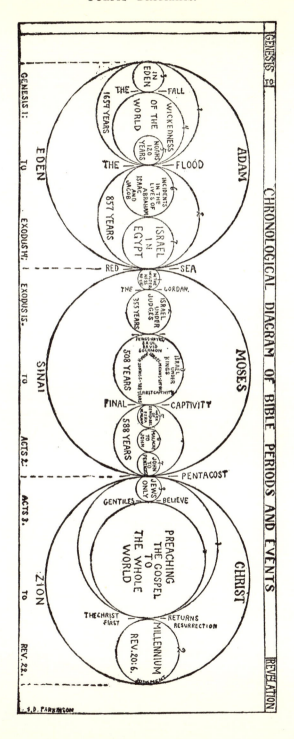

GENESIS TO CHRONOLOGICAL DIAGRAM OF BIBLE PERIODS AND EVENTS REVELATION

XV.—DIAGRAM OF THE BOOKS OF THE BIBLE.

GENESIS, written by Moses, B. C. 1491, contains history of the world from creation to Moses, and unfolds the Patriarchal or Gentile order of worship. While it was written by Moses, there is in it no law for the Jew; it is simply a partial account of what occurred before the Jews were a people expressly called out.

Moses' law to the Jews is found in Exodus to Deuteronomy, inclusive. These four books were not given to the world, but to the Jews only. The Ten Commandments, as such, were unknown until Moses received them at Sinai from the hand of God (Deut. v. 1–3).

Joshua to Esther, inclusive, contains a history of the execution of the Jewish law.

The Ten Commandments, found in Exodus, correspond to the Constitution of the United States; the statutes, found in Exodus to Deuteronomy, inclusive, to the statutes of the United States; and the history, found in Joshua to Esther, to the history of the United States. The books from Joshua to Esther, inclusive, are not law-books any more than the history of the United States is a law-book.

Job to Song of Solomon are poems, or religious songs, and were so used. Though instructive, they were not given to tell how to become Jew or Christian, nor how to live as such. They are not a rule of conduct to Gentile Jew nor Christian. They are the Hebrew Hymnology.

Following these poems are the writings of the greater prophets, five books, Isaiah to Daniel, then the lesser prophets, twelve books, Hosea to Malachi. They are not law, history nor hymnody; they are prophetic predictions. This closes the list of Old Testament books, but does not close the list of prophetic books, for immediately appeared John the Baptist, who was pronounced by Jesus the greatest prophet born of woman. John says of Jesus: "After me cometh a man who is preferred before me" (John i. 30). These two, then, were the greatest prophets of all the ages, and their prophecies were written by Matthew, Mark, Luke and John. These four books contain many parables and predictions relating to Christ and his church, given to none but the apostles to understand (Matt. xiii. 11). Christ bade them to take no money in their purses; to take but one coat; to take no thought for the morrow, nor what they should say, for in their hour of need it would be given them (Matt. x. 8–20). To others no such instructions were given. To the apostles he said: "Tarry in Jerusalem until ye be endowed with power from on high," then "Preach the gospel to every creature." In the end of each of these four books comes the cross. Before the cross there could be no gospel in fact. Before Adam the gospel was in the purpose of God; from Adam to Isaiah in the promise of God; from Isaiah to Malachi in the prophecy of God; from Matthew to John it was in preparation; in Acts it was preached by the apostles in fact.

The Book of Acts declares that Jesus, who was crucified and buried, has risen and ascended into the heavens, and is now both Lord and Christ, and that from this time to the end of the ages, obedience to him, according to the law of this book, will bring men and women into the church of God. This is the only book in the Bible that instances and records the exact order of this change. In every case of conversion narrated here, the apostles commenced by preaching to the people, and ended by immediately baptizing the converts into Christ. Between the preaching and baptisms they always enjoined heart belief in the Christ, repentance for past sins, and confession of the name of Jesus. Except in one case, Acts viii. 18–24, there were no instructions given to a single Christian.

From Romans to Jude we have twenty-one letters to the churches of Christ in which not one single command is given to a man not a Christian, but, in every case, instruction is given to Christians, telling them, not how to become Christians, but how to live as such. In every instance these letters are addressed to those already translated from the world into the church, to those who have already been baptized into Christ. Not a single command in any one of these epistles is given to unbelievers.

Revelation is a book of prophecy unfolding the future conflicts, defeats and victories of the church.

Account of Gentile or Patriarchal worship commences in Genesis, which worship continued to the preaching of the gospel. Account of Jewish worship commences in Exodus, which worship continued to the preaching of the gospel in Acts.

The first of these orders was the only worship the world knew for 2,513 years, when the second, which was quite unlike the first, was established, and the two ran parallel with each other for 1,524 years, when, by divine appointment, they both ceased on the day of Pentecost, A. D. 33, and the Gospel Age began, and will continue to the end of time.

Acts tell how to get from the world into the church.

The Epistles tell how to get from the church into heaven.

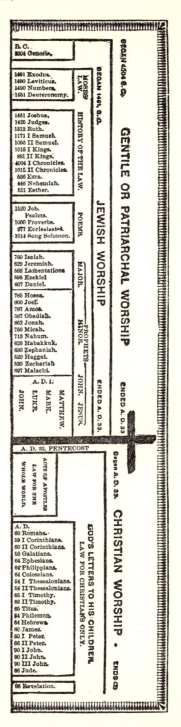

XVI.—THE GREAT SUN.

TEXT—Mal. iv. 2.

A BEAUTIFUL metaphor: the Sun of Righteousness compared to the sun of the solar system.

1. With the rising of the sun, a new day is ushered upon the material world. So with the advent of Christ, a new dispensation dawns upon the race (II. Cor. v. 17; Heb. x. 20). Types and shadows are obliterated (Heb. x. 1; iv. 12).

2. The sun is the brightest luminary in our planetary system. Likewise, Christ is the brightest, or *only* light in the spiritual world. He is "the fairest among ten thousand."

3. The sun is the source of all light. Scientists tell us that all combustible material, wood, coal, gas, and everything capable of producing light, is borrowed from the sun. This is true in the moral and spiritual world. "Without me, ye can do nothing" (Jno. xv. 5).

4. There could be no animal or vegetable life without the sun. Its obliteration, even for a brief period, would transform a tropical paradise into a frigid desolation. Death to everything would be inevitable. So John says, "He that hath the Son, hath life; he that hath not the Son of God, hath not life" (Jno. v. 12; also xiv. 6). "In him was life; and the life was the light of men" (Jno. i. 4).

5. The sun is a universal benefactor. It shines for all—the just and the unjust. So Christ's mission is a universal blessing. He "came to seek and to save the *lost*." He "came not to be ministered unto, but to minister." "I am come that they might have life."

6. The sun is the center of attraction. In it center the forces that hold the worlds in place—the centrifugal and centripetal forces. It is said that our planet (one of the smallest, too,) weighs six sextillion tons, yet it faithfully obeys its superior power. So Christ says, "All power is given me. If I be lifted up, I will draw all men unto me." He is the world's magnet.

7. Without the direct rays of the sun, there could be no vegetable development. So we may enjoy the light of the gospel, and yet, unless we have the Christ life *in* us, we shall not develop a strong, spiritual nature.

8. The sun bears his own evidence. It would be a foolish man who would undertake to prove the existence and power of the sun. Some are too blind to see the sun, but all who will, *may* see it. Likewise Christ's own life bears testimony to his superhuman power. His name can no more be obliterated from the world than the sun from his postion.

But we are asked why so many are not now under the influence of the world's great Sun? Christ answers this question himself in this language: "And this is the condemnation, that light is come into the world, and men loved darkness rather than light, *because* their deeds were evil" (Jno. iii. 19).

"And the light shineth in darkness; and the darkness comprehended it not."

"He is a sun and a shield."

"No good thing will he withhold from them that walk uprightly."

THE GREAT SUN

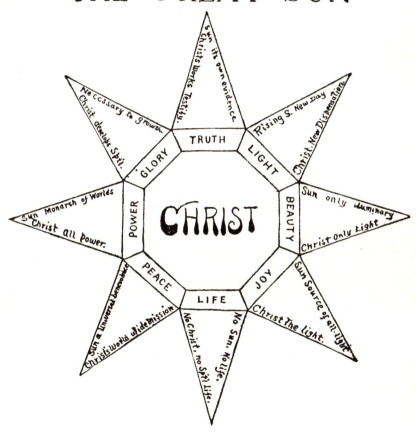

D. O. DARLING.

XVII.—THE ABRAHAMIC COVENANTS.

THE plan of salvation is comprehended in this little diagram.
    In the year 1921 B. C., God gave the great spiritual promise to Abraham; but he left it without conditions at that time, only renewing occasionally, to Isaac, Jacob, Joseph and David, etc.

About twelve years later, when Abraham was eighty-seven years old, in the year 1909 B. C., God again appeared to Abraham and made him the promise of the property covenant, or the land of Canaan. But God left this promise without condition at this time.

Then twenty-four years from the time God made the first promise, when Abraham was ninety-nine years old, in the year 1897 B. C., when Abraham was troubling himself about who his seed should be, God again appeared to him and gave him the covenant of circumcision, or the fleshly covenant. Then all who were circumcised were Abraham's heirs.

Now God had made these promises, and given them without condition. The promises were first a spiritual blessing; second, a property gift—real estate and personal property; and third, he had promised Abraham a seed —heirs. Then God gave the condition of the last covenant first, and the first last. They were circumcised to make them Abraham's heirs. Circumcision was the first condition.

The promise of the land of Canaan, or the property covenant, went four hundred and eighteen years without conditions. Then Moses became the mediator between God and Abraham's seed. Moses went from the promised land and told the Hebrews that the land was there, and God had promised it to them. After they were delivered from their Egyptian bondage, and when they came to Mt. Sinai, God called Moses up on the mountain to receive the conditions upon which they might possess that land. The conditions were given in the *Ten Commandments* about the year 1491 B. C.

The seed of Abraham were anxiously looking for the promised blessing through Abraham's seed, and they faithfully kept the covenant that made them Abraham's seed; and they were to some extent keeping the decalogue, or the law, which was added till that seed should come. When in the city of Bethlehem a child was born who was to redeem Israel and the world, and who was to be the mediator of a better covenant (the Spirit—the first) made upon better promises.

Moses, the mediator of the property, came from the country where the promises lay. Christ, the mediator of the spiritual covenant, came from the heavenly country where the great spiritual blessings await all the faithful.

Moses told Israel what they must do to possess the promised land, and so Christ, the great spiritual mediator, tells us the conditions upon which we may possess the spiritual blessings. He tells us what we must do to be saved from our sins; what we must do to become an heir of God, and what we must do to obtain eternal life.

They were Abraham's heirs by circumcision. They were disinherited for neglecting the conditions. They possessed the land of Canaan by keeping the Ten Commandments; they were driven off the land, or killed, when they violated the commandments.

We obtain the promises of the spiritual blessing by performing the conditions given by Christ, the mediator, in the New Testament. We will be condemned (Mark xvi. 16) and banished (II. Thess. i. 7) from God and the heavenly Canaan if we neglect the conditions (Heb. ii. 14).

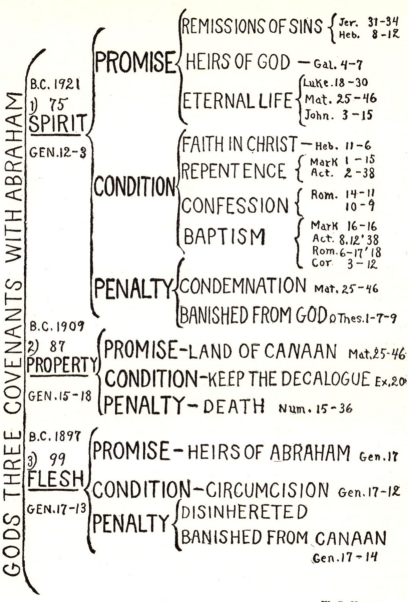

GODS THREE COVENANTS WITH ABRAHAM

1) B.C. 1921 75 SPIRIT GEN.12-3

- **PROMISE**
  - REMISSIONS OF SINS { Jer. 31-34 / Heb. 8-12
  - HEIRS OF GOD — Gal. 4-7
  - ETERNAL LIFE { Luke.18-30 / Mat. 25-46 / John. 3-15
- **CONDITION**
  - FAITH IN CHRIST — Heb. 11-6
  - REPENTENCE { Mark 1-15 / Act. 2-38
  - CONFESSION { Rom. 14-11 / 10-9
  - BAPTISM { Mark 16-16 / Act. 8.12'38 / Rom. 6-17'18 / Cor. 3-12
- **PENALTY**
  - CONDEMNATION Mat. 25-46
  - BANISHED FROM GOD 2 Thes.1-7-9

2) B.C. 1909 87 PROPERTY GEN.15-18

- PROMISE—LAND OF CANAAN Mat.25-46
- CONDITION—KEEP THE DECALOGUE Ex.20
- PENALTY—DEATH Num. 15-36

3) B.C. 1897 99 FLESH GEN.17-13

- PROMISE—HEIRS OF ABRAHAM Gen.17
- CONDITION—CIRCUMCISION Gen.17-12
- PENALTY { DISINHERETED / BANISHED FROM CANAAN Gen.17-14

W. C. HIGGINS.

XVIII.—The Three Great Religions of the Bible.

TEXT—Heb. i. 1, 2.

AT THE left on my chart is a column supporting an arch, which is ETERNITY. It represents that eternity out of which TIME sprang, and of which we know nothing. It is in darkness.

At the right of my chart is another column supporting another arch, which is ETERNITY. It represents the eternity to which we look. To the child of God and follower of Jesus it is bright.

The space between is TIME, and the figures represent that TIME in spaces of 500 years each. The infidel can not see anything beyond time. He has no light. We have—THE BIBLE.

The *rainbow* spanning TIME and reaching from one eternity to the other, represents RELIGION. God has never left man without religion.

But God has not always given man the same religion. Beginning at the first, an arch spans 2,500 years: From the Fall to Sinai. This is the PATRIARCHAL religion. The ALTAR was its place and form of worship. In this time occurred the Flood; Call of Abram; Going into Egypt, and other events.

God saw fit in time to take this away and give another religion. Beginning from Sinai, another arch spans 1,500 years, reaching from Sinai to the Cross. This is the JEWISH religion. In this occurs the Giving of the LAW, Sabbath, Tabernacle, Possession of Canaan, Temple, Prophets, John the Baptist, and Personal Ministry of Christ.

God took this away also, giving another religion. Beginning at the cross is another arch, which fades away in the rainbow, and will some day reach eternity. There will be no more change. This is the CHRISTIAN religion.

The stars in the PATRIARCHAL, the moon in the JEWISH, and the sun in the CHRISTIAN show us the increasing light, and that we have now reached the perfect light: the full light of the Sun. They are the starlight, moonlight, and sunlight ages of the world.

Under the Christian religion, and immediately after the Cross, is the Descent of the Holy Spirit; First Preaching of the Gospel; First Christians Made; The Church Born; Christian Baptism; The Lord's Supper; The Lord's Day; Prayer in the Name of Jesus. The table of stone with Ten Commandments leaning over " JEWISH," and the Bible open at the division between Old Testament and New Testament, with Old Testament toward JEWISH and PATRIARCHAL, and New Testament toward CHRISTIAN, indicate the relation of each to the religions.

FAITH on one column, and HOPE on the other, are very expressive.

Any event in Bible history may be located on this chart, and its place in history and its relation to God and men known.

XIX.—WHAT IS CAMPBELLISM?

EXPLANATION.

THE Church of Christ began on Pentecost, in the year A. D. 29. "The sacred writings were the only symbol known to the primitive church, and that was the most saintly and successful period of Christianity. They paused not in their mighty and aggressive work to define, in an authoritative way, dogmatic formulas" (*Church History*). Scripture to read: Matt. xvi. 18; Acts ii. 47; Acts xi. 26. There was but one church, and the members of it were known by the general title, Christians.

2. In the beginning of the fourth century a great controversy arose about the nature of Christ between Alexander and Arias, two distinguished Presbyters, and a great council was called by Constantine, the Roman Emperor, and three hundred and eighteen bishops met at Nice in A. D. 325, and made the Nicene Creed, to which they required adhesion as well as to the Bible. Out of this grew what is to-day known as the Roman Catholic Church.

3. At the beginning of the sixteenth century Martin Luther challenged the claims of the Roman Catholic Church, and once more made the Bible the supreme test. At the Diet of Worms he made the contest and the contrast and aroused all Germany. His coadjutors were afraid to trust the Bible alone, so they wrote out a creed which was adopted at Augsburg in 1530, and on it was erected what is known as the Lutheran Church, and the members known by the general title of Lutherans.

4. About the same time King Henry VIII., of England, was married to Catharine of Aragon, the aunt of Charles V. of Spain. King Henry fell in love with Anna Boleyn, a waiting-maid of Catharine, and asked the Pope to grant him a divorce from Catharine, that he might marry Anna. The Pope, out of deference to Charles V., delayed the matter until Henry took the matter into his own hands, declared himself divorced from Catharine and married Anna, and taking his place at the head of the church, appointed Bishop Cranmer to prepare the creed,which was adopted in 1552, and became the basis of the Protestant Episcopal Church, the members of it being known by the general title of Episcopalians.

3. King Charles I., one of the successors of King Henry, quarreled with his Parliament, who refused to obey his order, and so they levied war against him, and in order to secure the support of the independents and followers of John Calvin, they authorized them to make a creed. So a council was called of one hundred and twenty clergymen, twenty peers, and ten commoners, and they spent two years in making what is known as the Westminster Confession of Faith. They met in 1643, and that confession became, in addition to the Bible, the creed of the Presbyterian Church, the members of it being known by the general title of Presbyterians.

6. Benedict's History, page 304, says: "The first Baptist Church of which we have any account is dated from London in 1607, and was found by a Mr. Smyth, who had been a clergyman of the Church of England." The first Baptist Church in this country was organized in Rhode Island by Roger Williams and Ezekiel Hollaman, but whether the main body of the Baptists came from England or from Rhode Island is a question, but an association in Philadelphia, in 1742, adopted a confession that was generally recognized, and the members known by the general title of Baptists.

7. The history of the Methodist Episcopal Church, started in Methodist Societies by John Wesley, is so familiar that it is only necessary to say that a general conference in 1784 cut down the thirty-nine articles to twenty-five, and gave us the M. E. creed and discipline in addition to the Bible, and the members are known by the general title of Methodists.

8. At the beginning of this century a man by the name of Thomas Campbell, looking back over the past, and seeing the war of creeds that had grown up, suggested as a remedy for the strife and division that they go back and reproduce the primitive church with its creed, its rules, and its practice. In order to do this, he presented the maxim of the line across the base of the diagram, "Where the Bible speaks, we speak, and where the Bible is silent, we are silent." That was the principle presented and acted upon by Thomas Campbell and his son, Alexander Campbell, and the first church organized upon that basis was in 1823, with the Bible as foundation, known as the Church of Christ, or Christian Church, and the members of it by the general title of Christians.

WHAT IS CAMPBELLISM.

BY D.R. LUCAS.

A.D. 29	325	1530	1552	1643	1742	1784	1823
CHRISTIANS	CATHOLICS	LUTHERANS	EPISCOPALIANS	PRESBYTERIANS	BAPTISTS	METHODISTS	CHRISTIANS
THE CHURCH OF CHRIST	ROMAN CATHOLIC CHURCH	LUTHERAN CHURCH	PROTESTANT EPISCOPAL CHURCH	PRESBYTERIAN CHURCH	BAPTIST CHURCH	METHODIST EPISCOPAL CHURCH	THE CHURCH OF CHRIST
	NICENE CREED	AUGSBURG CREED	EPISCOPAL CREED	WESTMINSTER CREED	PHILADELPHIA CREED	M.E. CREED AND DISCIPLINE	
BIBLE	BIBLE	BIBLE	BIBLE	BIBLE	BIBLE	BIBLE	BIBLE

"WHERE THE BIBLE SPEAKS, WE SPEAK AND WHERE THE BIBLE IS SILENT WE ARE SILENT." = THIS IS CAMPBELLISM.

D. R. LUCAS.

XX.—THE DESTINIES OF MAN.

["*Behold, I set before you the way of life, and the way of death.*"—Jer. xxi. 8.]

THUS spoke the weeping prophet at the bidding of Jehovah to the renegade nation of Jews twenty-four centuries ago ; so speaks the divine will in the Scriptures to the world to-day. All are confronted with one of two destinies. The diagram represents all the possibilities and conditions of human existence, from feeblest to highest intellectual glory ; from deepest moral degradation to loftiest spiritual joy.

I. THE WORLD OUR STARTING-POINT.

1. Innocent infancy the first condition. Over one-half the race said to die in this stage. All such, by virtue of Christ's death, and his gracious promise implied in Matt. xix. 14, pass through the gate of death (D. 2) to glory and heaven.

2. The second class dwelling in the world, who live up to the light of their moral natures, but have no opportunity to hear or know the gospel, we may place with those Gentiles of whom Paul speaks in Rom. ii. 14, 15. No heathens are lost for disobedience to the gospel till they have a chance for salvation through it, and reject that opportunity.

3. The third and lagest class familiar to us is that of sinners. Rebels against God's will, despisers of his love, and neglecters of his mercy. But some—many, thank God!—see their danger ere too deeply sunk in the *blackness* of sin, and seek salvation in God's own way. Those who live and die in disobedience pass through the gate of death (D. 4) into the lost world. (The judgment impends, but they are none the less lost.)

II. THE UPLIFTED CROSS.

The symbol and emblem of all-saving love stands in full view of the sinner, and through it a pathway is made by conversion (C.) to a better life and hope.

All who convert in full surrender to the personal authority of Jesus by obedience to his gospel, are thereby brought into

III. THE CHURCH OF CHRIST,

And are Christians, unless they choose to be hypocrites. An apology is due for placing the hypocrite in this square. He seems to be in the church ; but it is only seeming. He has only taken the long way round to go to perdition in company with the backslider who has forgotten the first pardon of sins, and will receive no more for lack of repentance. Both pass into hell through the gate of death (D. 3). But heaven is possible till hell is entered—then the great gulf is fixed. In the church of Christ true children of God strive to rise above the dark lines of doubt and unfaithfulness into the clear light of "full assurance." The cross is still in full view. Upward is toward life, downward is death. Which way, brother ? The Christian must die ; the mere churchman must die, and the gates are open. Through the upper gate of death (D. 1) the true saint passes to

IV. HEAVEN, THE HOME OF THE SOUL.

There is the beautiful gate, the jasper wall, the crystal river, the harps attuned, the flashing crowns. This destiny is glorious ; prepared of God ; purchased by the love and blood of Jesus. The cross uplifted to heaven lifts us to heaven. The crown above is won by it. Without the cross that crown can not be attained.

REFLECTIONS.

1. Can not one go to heaven without Christ's Church ? Yes, by dying in infancy, or by having no opportunity to hear the gospel, and by loyally living up to the moral nature (Rom. ii. 14, 15).

2. A man is not a moralist who hears and disobeys the gospel. He rejects the highest morality. A moralist is one who can have no law but his own moral nature. There are none such in Christian lands, and not many anywhere.

3. As the sinner goes deeper and deeper into the world, his character and hope come into great darkness. He can not go back to child-purity, but may find pardon at the cross.

4. Is there no promise for death-bed repentance ? None whatever, as such a thing does not exist. Dying persons may sorrow, but can not repent. There is no *promise*, but God may save without. Dare we rely on that ?

5. We pass into the Church of Christ and into the promises by way of the cross. "He that climbeth up some other way is a thief and robber."

6. All (nominally) in the church are not Christians, nor is church membership a passport to heaven. The devil delights to populate his kingdom with counterfeit Christians.

7 Hell is beneath the cross. Christ is putting all enemies under his feet.

8. The cross pierces heaven, and adds to its glory. "God forbid that I should glory save in the cross of our Lord Jesus Christ."

9. Hell grows blacker in its extreme depths. Not all are in the same degree of sin. "According to their works" is punishment and reward.

Two destinies—Life and Death—at the end of two ways—obedience and disobedience. Which way, O mortal man ?

THE DESTINIES of MAN
~ JER. XXI: 8 ~

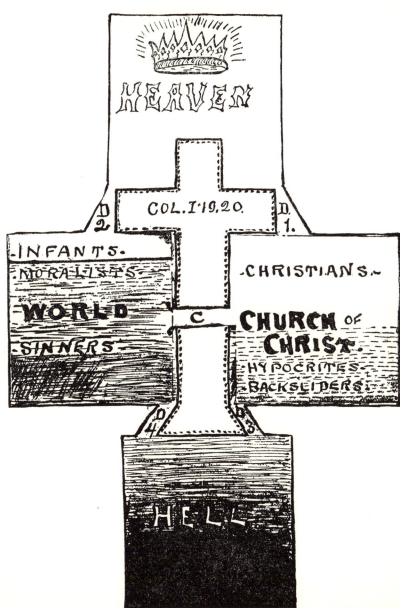

E. O. SHARPE.

XXI.—THE GREAT COMMISSION.

THE subject of this diagram is Christ's commission for the conversion of the world.

2. *A commission is an instrument conferring authority upon a minister.* Illustrate by the United States Ministers sent to foreign courts. Within the limits of their commission they have all power; outside of it, none.

3. *The last commission given by him.* It is a principle of legislation that a recent enactment repeals all previous conflicting legislation. So if there should be found, previous to this commission, that which seems to conflict, it is thereby repealed.

4. *It is the only world-embracing one.* He had given others, but they were partial, individual, or national; but this is the first universal commission. All the authority for gospel work lies in this. Contrast this with the absurd "calls" men have claimed to receive.

5. *It is the reproductive principle of Christianity.* As the aloe plant toils for ninety-nine years that on the hundredth it may shoot up one spike of glory, "and thus the energies sublime of a century burst full blossomed from the thorny stem of time," so God worked four thousand years that Jesus might be brought forth. Then he labored for thirty-three years, and then gave this commandment and was taken up into glory. If this "commandment" had not been given, no gospel would have been preached; none believed; no conversions; no church; no Epistles; no "Acts"; no New Testament.

6. *Very important that we understand this commission.* (*a*) The preacher might fail to carry it out. (*b*) He might seek to pervert it. Preachers have been known to do both these things.

7. A note from Matthew, Mark, Luke and John, and we have five items: (1) Teaching; (2) Faith; (3) Repentance; (4) Baptism; (5) Salvation. Everybody believes all these items are in the commission, but we differ as to arrangement. Arrangement is a very important thing, as can be illustrated by arranging the four letters, L I V E, in different ways.

8. The arrangement of these items in the first gospel sermon ever preached by the first called, qualified and sent preacher of the gospel, on the day of Pentecost, ought to forever settle the matter of arrangement.

The Gospels set forth the first clause; Acts of Apostles, the second clause; the Epistles, the third clause; Revelation, the fourth clause.

THE GREAT COMMISSION

	GO	
MATH.		Teach -- Baptize
MARK		Preach Believe Baptize Saved
LUKE		Repentance and Remission
JOHN		Nothing Additional
ALL FOUR		Teach Baptize Believe Saved Repentance

DIFFERENT ARRANGEMENTS

PAIDOBAPTIST | 1) Baptism 2) Teaching 3) Repentance 4) Faith 5) Salvation

BAPTIST | 1) Teaching 2) Repentance 3) Faith 4) Salvation 5) Baptism

CHRISTIAN | 1) Teaching 2) Faith 3) Repentence 4) Baptism 5) Salvation

IMPORTANCE OF PROPER ARRANGEMENT
Illustrated by the four letters LIVE
1) LIVE 2) EVIL 3) VEIL 4) VILE

ARRANGEMENTS OF HOLY SPIRIT AT PENTACOST
1) TEACHING 2) FAITH 3) REPENTANCE
4) BAPTISM 5) SALVATION

MATH. MARK LUKE JOHN = "All authority in Heaven and Earth"
ACTS = "Preach Gospel to every creature"
EPISTLES = "Teaching to observe all things."
REVELATION = Lo I am with you always.

XXII.—THE COVENANTS.

THE cross is placed between the two covenants to show that the old covenant ended in the cross, and the new began with it. It divided and united the two dispensations.
"Behold, the days come, saith the Lord, that I will make a new covenant with the house of Israel and the house of Judah; not according to the covenant that I made with their fathers in the day I took them by the hand to lead them out of the land of Egypt" (Jer. xxxi. 31, 32).
It is our purpose to show the chief points of difference between these two covenants.
The first covenant was made with the children of Israel at Mt. S.nai. Moses was the mediator. In his farewell address to Israel he said, "The Lord our God made a covenant with us in Horeb. The Lord made not this covenant with our fathers, but with us, who are all alive here this day" (Deut. v. 2, 3). This covenant was sealed with the blood of beasts. For when Moses had spoken every commandment to all the people according to the Law, he took the blood of calves and of goats with water and scarlet wool and sprinkled both the book and all the people, saying, this is the blood of the covenant which God hath commanded you (Heb. ix. 19, 20).
The new covenant was made with the people of Israel, and was designed for all nations. Jesus was the mediator. But now hath he obtained a more excellent ministry, by how much also he is the mediator of a better covenant, which was established upon better promises (Heb. viii. 6). It was sealed with his blood: "For this is my blood of the new covenant, which is shed for many for the remission of sins" (Matt. xxvi. 28). It began in Jerusalem among the Jews, and was to be offered to all nations. And he said unto them, "Thus it is written, and thus it behooved the Christ to suffer, and to rise from the dead the third day, and that repentance and remission of sins should be preached in his name among all nations, beginning from Jerusalem" (Luke xxiv. 46, 47; Matt. xxviii. 19, 20).
The old covenant was also called the *Law.* It was a system of worship of Jehovah, and of ad ministration of justice among the people. The new covenant is called the gospel, for it is the good news of salvation for all men through Jesus Christ (John i. 17).
The first covenant was written on tables of stone, the second on fleshly tables of the heart (II. Cor. iii. 3). "I will put my laws into their mind and write them in their hearts" (Jer. xxxi. 33).
The first covenant is called "the ministration of death," for it brought death upon all who broke it. The second is called "the ministration of the spirit," for it offered life to all who accepted it. The first was "the ministration of condemnation," the second "the ministration of righteousness," or justification (II. Cor. iii. 6-9). The glory of the first may be compared to the light of the moon; the glory of the second, to the light of the sun.
The first covenant was based on *works.* The man which doeth these things shall live by them (Lev. xviii. 5). The second covenant is a system of *faith.* Know that a man is not justified by the works of the law, but by the faith of Jesus Christ; even we have believed in Jesus Christ, that we might be justified by the faith of Christ, and not by the works of the law; for by the works of the law shall no flesh be justified (Gal. ii. 16; iii. 23, 24).
The first covenant could not give full pardon for sins. For the law having a shadow of good things to come, *and* not the very image of the things, can never with those sacrifices which they offered year by year, continually make the comers thereunto perfect. For it is not possible that the blood of bulls and of goats should take away sins (Heb. x. 1, 4). There was forgiveness under the law for sins of error, ignorance, and ceremonial uncleanness, but not for sins of the conscience, or violations of the moral law, or ten commandments.
But the new covenant offers forgiveness to all who accept it. I will forgive their iniquities, and I will remember their sins no more (Jer. xxxi. 34). For if the blood of bulls and of goats, and the ashes of an heifer sprinkling the unclean, purifieth the *flesh:* how much more shall the blood of Christ, who through the eternal Spirit offered himself without spot to God, cleanse your conscience from dead works to serve the living God? (Heb. xi. 12, 13). The blood of Christ was shed for the remission of sins under the first covenant as well as for those under the second covenant (Heb. ix. 15).
Circumcision was a mark of distinction upon the members of the old covenant. It drew the line between the Jews and Gentiles. It was first given to Abraham (Gen. xvii. 9-14) and afterwards incorporated into the covenant of Sinai (Lev. xii. 3; Josh. v.). It was typical of the putting away of sins under the gospel (Col. ii. 11).
Baptism is the ordinance of the new covenant which separates its members from the world. Ye are all the children of God by faith in Christ Jesus, for as many of you as have been baptized into Christ, have put on Christ (Gal. iii. 26, 27). It is the boundary line between the world and the kingdom of God (John iii. 5). It is one of the conditions of the forgiveness of sins (Acts ii. 38; Mark xv. 16); the last step in the process by which persons become members of the new covenant (Rom. vi. 3, 4).
Under the first covenant infants became members by circumcision when eight days old, and afterwards were taught the knowledge of God. Under the new covenant none can become a member until he has the knowledge of God. And they shall not teach every man his neighbor and his brother, saying, Know the Lord, for they shall all know me, from the least of them to the greatest of them, saith the Lord (Jer. xxxi. 34; also John vi. 45). Infants will be saved, because not sinners.
The keeping of the Sabbath was made obligatory upon all the members of the covenant: first, because God had rested on that day from his work (Ex. xx. 11). Second, because God had delivered his people from the bondage of Egypt (Deut. v. 15). It was never bound upon any other nation except the Jews, therefore no other nation is obliged to keep it. It was a shadow of things to come (Col. ii. 16, 17), and the law concerning it was repealed at the death of Christ (Rom. vii. 4-6).
The first day of the week, or Lord's day, commemorates the resurrection of Jesus Christ, and should be observed by all the members of the new covenant, not by reason of a positive command, but from the example of the apostles and early Christians (John xx. 19; Acts xx. 7; I. Cor. xvi, 2). The *genius* of the new institution demands it, the honor of its Founder, and the good of his people.
The Passover was given to the Jewish people as a memorial of their deliverance from Egypt (Ex. xii. 12-14: Deut. xvi. 1-3), and they were commanded to keep it throughout all their generations.
The Lord's Supper is a memorial of the deliverance of Christ's people from the bondage of sin. For even Christ, our passover, is sacrificed for us (I. Cor. v. 7). It was given by the Lord Jesus to his apostles, and by them given to the churches which they established under the new covenant (I. Cor. xi. 23-25), and should be observed as a perpetual memorial of his death until he comes again (I. Cor. xi. 26). We believe it should be kept on every first day of the week (Acts xx. 7). The first covenant was temporal, the second eternal. The object of giving the first was to educate the people and prepare them for the coming of Christ, and then its mission was ended (Gal. iii. 19, 24, 25).

Christ came to fulfill the law and the prophets (Luke xxiv. 44). He came not to *destroy* the law, but to *fulfill* it (Matt. v. 17). It was fulfilled at his death. When he said it, "It is finished," the law came to an end (Eph. ii. 14, 15; Col. ii 14). For if that which was done away [the old covenant] was glorious, much more that which remaineth [the new covenant] is glorious (II. Cor. iii. 11; Heb. viii. 13). The reason is given (Heb. vii. 18, 19). The new covenant came into operation on the day of Pentecost after Christ's ascension (Acts ii.). The covenant is eternal (Heb. xiii. 20; v. 8, 9). The blessings and curses under the first covenant were temporal (Deut. xxviii. 1-20). The rewards and punishments under the new covenant are eternal (Matt. xxv. 46; Rom. ii. 6-11).

THE COVENANTS

OLD COVENANT	NEW COVENANT
MOSES	CHRIST
THE LAW	THE GOSPEL
MT. SINAI	MT. ZION
ONE NATION	ALL NATIONS
WORKS	FAITH
FLESH	SPIRIT
CIRCUMCISION	BAPTISM
SABBATH	LORDS DAY
EARTHLY	HEAVENLY
TEMPORAL	ETERNAL

J. H. GORDINIER.

XXIII.—THE DEVELOPMENT OF REDEMPTION.

STUDY OF THE DIAGRAM.

MAN innocent in Eden.
2. Man fallen through sin.
3. Redemption begun; sacrifice instituted; an altar built.
4. Men classified on the basis of faith (Heb. xi. 4).
5. Unbelieving world destroyed by flood; Noah saved by faith.
6. The old classification continued in the New World.
7. Abraham called "the father of all them that believe" (Rom. iv. 11).
8. A new distinction is introduced: Abraham's Seed *vs.* The Nation; Circumcision *vs.* Uncircumcision. Based on the flesh.
9. This distinction given corporate definition and emphasis by the formation of Abraham's "seed" into a nation. Thenceforth the terms "Israel" and "the Gentiles" describe humanity.
10. Sinai, the birthplace of the *nation* of Israel.
11. The "old covenant" between God and *the nation of Israel;* the "law" given to Israel with its service and sanctuary; the promises entrusted to Israel. "Whose is the adoption and the glory, and the covenants, and the giving of the law, and the service, and the promises," etc. (Rom. ix. 4). The "Gentiles" "have no law" (Rom. ii. 14). They were alienated from the commonwealth of Israel, strangers from the covenants of promise, having no hope and without God in the world (Eph. ii. 12). Yet, perchance, doing by nature the things of the law; being a law unto themselves; shewing the work of the law written in their hearts; having the witness of conscience, etc. (Rom. ii. 14, 15).
12. The cross of Christ stands in the middle of the ages. There old things are fulfilled and pass away. Sacrificial offerings, the old covenant—law—"letter"—end there. Distinctions based on the flesh end there. There is to be no more "Jew" and "Gentile." The middle wall of partition broken down. One new man to be made out of the *two.*
13. As the cross stands for the end of the old, it stands for the beginning of the new. A new covenant; a new message—the gospel; a new power of life—the Spirit; a new institution—the church.
14. The "faith line," which runs throughout the Patriarchal and Jewish dispensations, comes down through the cross, and in the Christian dispensation emerges into a *faith institution*—the church. Jew and Gentile, without distinction, come into the church on the basis of faith, their differences abolished at the cross. In Christ "there can be neither Jew nor Greek" (Gal. iii. 28). When in Christ, Jew and Gentile are "Abraham's seed and heirs acccording to the promise" (Gal. iii. 29).
15. The cross *divides* the ages; faith *unites* them.
16. Pentecost is to the new age what Sinai was to the old.
17. There are but two states: Christ (church); the world. Every man in one or the other; no middle ground. The church, Christ's body, the medium through which God brings men back to Eden purity, and developes them into heavenly perfection.
18. The cross reaches down to the depths of lost humanity, up to the heights of Eden innocence; back to the first lost soul, forward to the last sinner.

"In the cross of Christ I glory,
Towering o'er the wrecks of time;
All the light of sacred story
Gathers round its head sublime."

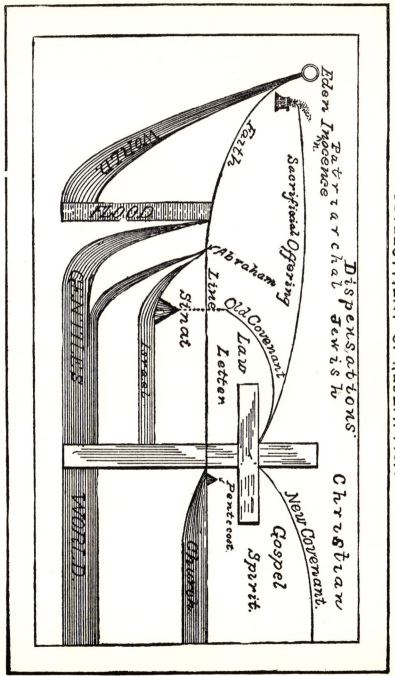

DEVELOPMENT OF REDEMPTION

M. B. Ryan.

XXIV.—MOSES AND SCIENCE.

THE AUTHORSHIP OF THE PENTATEUCH.—We assume Moses to be the author of the "five-fold book" which reaches from Genesis to Deuteronomy. That he may have drawn from earlier documents in portions of his work, and that the books may have been revised and retouched by Ezra, we may perhaps safely admit.

HISTORY OF THE BOOKS.—1. That the Pentateuch was in existence in its present form in the time of Christ, and was attributed by him and his contemporaries to Moses, needs no argument. As far back as the time of Ezra, B. C. 444, there is no dispute, and no claim of modification. 2. It is when we pass beyond this date and attempt to identify the Pentateuch, as in the days of Josiah, B. C. 640, that its integrity is disputed. The reputed finding of the Book of the Law, as recorded in II. Kings xxii. 8. and II. Chron. xxxiv. 14–21, is discredited, and the work is assumed to have been manufactured for the occasion. This important conclusion rests mainly on the ground that it would have been impossible for a book of such importance to be so lost; and the accidental finding of the work just at a time when it met the needs of the reformers (among whom Jeremiah was a chief), suggests to some men the idea of forgery. But it simply is not strange that under the grossly idolatrous reigns just preceding, the books should have been lost; nor would it be unlikely that those who sought earnestly to restore a pure worship should be the ones to find them. 3. Isaiah and others in the eighth century, B. C., contain numerous allusions to the story of the Pentateuch, and the harmony of tone is too complete not to be taken from it. The same may be said of the Psalms of David written two centuries earlier. Indeed, who can read the loftiest Psalms and fail to believe that our "books of Moses" lay under them? The writer of the 27th and the 103rd Psalms must naturally have been to school to the great Law-giver; the writer of the 78th most certainly so. 4. Under Samuel and the judges the methods of administration, and the efforts to maintain a theocratic form of government, argue for the existence of the Pentateuch. And so we come back to the days of Joshua, in whose history references to the Book of the Law of Moses are so frequent (i. 7, 8; xxiii. 6, etc.) that those who oppose the Mosaic origin of the Pentateuch add this book to the five, and attribute to them all a common origin.

There always will be those who prefer to leave the solid and sensible mainland of truth that they may go a-sailing on the wide ocean in quest of what they have left behind. There seems to us no reason for displacing Moses from that place which in the mind of the Christian world, he so long has filled. As the Christian Church can not be explained unless we see back of it Christ and the apostolic gospels, no more can the whole history of the Jewish Church be understood unless we see back of all Moses and the Pentateuch.

THE STORY OF CREATION.—The most rational explanation of the existing order of things is that which the Bible gives. Only three conceptions are possible : 1. All things have forever existed as they now do. 2. The universe, with its wondrous order, and this world, with its diverse and yet unified life, have all come by chance. 3. The present system has been developed according to a steadfast plan, and under uniform laws. But this last hypothesis (which is the only one the enlightened reason can for a moment accept) is impossible and unthinkable, unless we accept an intelligent Designer and Law giver—a Great Creator. Without troubling ourselves at present to adjust every item, we may say that there is a marvelous agreement between nature and the Bible in the bolder and more general outlines of the story of creation. A diagram may illustrate at least a possible parallelism :

CREATION IN GENESIS AND GEOLOGY.					
Days.	Genesis i.	Geology.	Ages.	Geologic Times.	Group of Rocks.
1.	Verses 1-3. Creation of matter. Chaos. Light.	Igneous vapor condensing. Matter cooling and taking form.	Age of Fire.	Azoic.	Metamorphic Granite.
2.	Verses 5-8. Creation of firmament.	Gathering of clouds; descent of rain; first sediment.	Age of Rain.		Pottsdam. Trenton. Niagara.
3.	Verses 9 13. Creation of dry land and plants.	Uplifting of continents, and first plants. Lowest forms of all life.	Age of Land and Plant making	Paleozoic.	Limestone. Old Red Sandstone.
4.	Verses 14-19. Sun and stars called forth.	Clouds condense and break, and sun and stars appear.	Age of Plant growth.		Coal Measures. Limestone.
5.	Verses 20-23. Aquatics, and birds.	Marine animals, fishes and birds. "Great sea monsters."	Age of Mollusks, Fishes, Reptiles and Birds.	Mesozoic.	Lias. Chalk.
6.	Verses 24-31. Land, animals and man.	Mammals and man.	Age of Mammals.	Cenozoic.	Eocene. Miocene. Pliocene. Alluvial Drift.
7.	Gen. ii. 2, 3. Lord rested. Creation ended.	Since man came, no new species of life.	Age of Man.	Phrenozoic.	Soil.

XXV.—"BIBLE PLAN OF SALVATION."

MUCH has been said concerning the question, "What shall I do to be saved?" and, with growing interest, it is still agitated. It is evident that, with most of those discussing the matter, there is an intense desire to know the truth, and that the question will be agitated until a simplicity is reached that will satisfy the most confused. Accordingly, we have been reading the various articles, extracts, etc., with much interest, endeavoring to simplify the question for our own satisfaction. In the diagram we submit a digest of our investigations, inviting the most serious consideration of the points involved. Not for controversy, but for the elucidation of truth, we prayerfully submit the following. (See diagram on opposite page.)

First, we have a statement of the proposition in the arrangement of the columns and the circle, as indicated by the Scriptures. The several columns, eleven in all, representing the entire response to the question, "What shall I do to be saved?"—the circle cutting these columns where the Scriptures direct, making a proper distinction between first and second principles; the latter *within* the circle, *in Christ;* the former without, approaching Christ.

In the s.atement we assume that faith, repentance, confession and baptism constitute the direct response to the question as to the conditions of pardon to the alien; assuming this, we institute an examination and comparison of the several cases of conversion, as recorded in the Acts of the Apostles, specifying the terms of pardon wherever expressed, substituting a dash wherever omitted. Having thus canvassed and arranged the facts as they occur, we then sum them up in their respective columns. Thus we have in the result what we assumed in the statement of the proposition—faith, repentance, confession and baptism, as conditions of pardon to the alien. However, in looking over these columns, we find faith specified but three times, in the words "believed" and "believe"; repentance twice; confession once, and baptism seven times, in eight cases of clearly defined conversions under the great commission. Two important questions are suggested here: First, why these omissions? Secondly, why does "baptism" occur in every case but one? Now, this necessitates a brief consideration of the second phase of our question, viz.: demonstration. But it is not so much our purpose to discuss the matter as to suggest, by reference, points of vital interest, leaving the reader to consult the Scriptures as to whether the things to which we refer "be so or not." In doing so, you will discover that specifications and omissions occur according to the education, condition of the mind and heart of the parties, and circumstances attendant upon them—*e. g.*, Acts ii. 38, in the context it is said they cried out: "Men and brethren, what shall we do?" Thus their faith appears, and, virtually, confession of the name of Jesus, against whom they had sinned. They were required to call on the name of the Lord. (See v. 21.) Acts iii. 19, Peter evidently addressed a people who had heard him only a little while before, on Pentecost. In the word "repent" faith is implied, and it is not inconsistent with facts *even thus far developed*, to believe that confession was made. For it was through faith in his name that the man lame was made whole (v. 16). How much more vital his name in the healing of the soul! In the phrase "be converted," baptism is also implied; certainly we can not say it *is not*, because omitted, for then the frequent omission of faith and repentance would make it appear that *they were* not required. Acts viii. 12: "When they believed Philip preaching the things concerning the kingdom of God and the name of Jesus Christ, they were baptized, both men and women." Certainly repentance is implied, inasmuch as they believed. Philip preached *the name* of Jesus Christ. It is reasonable to infer that they confessed the name *as* it was preached. Thus they were baptized, both men and women.

Acts viii. 37: In the response of Philip, "If thou believest with all thy heart thou mayest," most assuredly repentance is implied, and in the answer of the eunuch we have the confession.

Acts x. 48: Again, faith, repentance and confession included (see v. 43).

Acts xvi. 15: The same evidently required (v. 14).

Acts xvi. 31, 33: Here Paul propounds the same question—in different words, however—to the jailor that Philip did to the eunuch; and is it unreasonable to suppose that the jailor made the same confession, though in different words? Acts xxii. 16, Paul's own conversion, faith, repentance and confession appear. He, and all others, not only require to believe and repent, but to confess, or call on the name of the Lord, making them fit subjects for baptism, in the name of the Father, the Son and the Holy Spirit.

Reaching this, or the sinner thus obeying, what of the result? 1. In Christ. 2. Pardon. 3. Gift of the Spirit. These results represented in the circle; also thus in the Scriptures. (See references).

On further examination you will observe that the New Testament authorizes the order of Pardon, Gift of Spirit, Christian Graces, Sins and Result as arranged in the columns within the circle.

In regard to pardon and gift of the Spirit, in first two columns, we have several omissions, but it will appear at once, without special investigation, that they are implied. Now, in order to the final triumph of the believer, being born again, being a new creature in *Christ Jesus*, let him add the graces specified, and observe *law* of *pardon* for *the believer*, as indicated in the column (sins); he will realize the blessings of last column (result), victory and crown, through faith in our Lord Jesus Christ, to the glory of God the Father.

In upper arc of the circle you will notice the phrase, "*In Christ;*" in lower arc, "*All is yea and amen.*" This *Christ idea* fills the circle. With the data thus before us, with the following questions, we submit the diagram, with its arrangement, on its own merits.

First. Is it possible to write the grand declaration, "All things in Christ Jesus are yea and amen," on the outside of the circle and retain its significance?

Second. Can the circle be readjusted so as to include *more* or *less*, without doing violence to the general teachings of the apostles under the great commission?

Third. If neither of these things can be done, have we not a uniform and a clearly defined response to the alien, "*What to do to be saved;*" or how to attain eternal life?

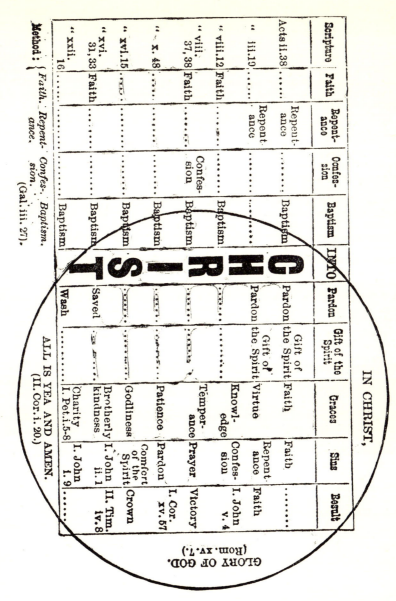

Scripture	Faith	Repent-ance	Confes-sion	Baptism	INTO	Pardon	Gift of the Spirit	Graces	Sins	Result
Acts ii.38	......	Repent-ance	......	Baptism		Pardon	Gift of the Spirit	Faith	Faith	......
" iii.19	......	Repent-ance	......			Pardon	Gift of the Spirit	Virtue	Repent-ance	Faith
" viii.12	Faith	......	......	Baptism		Pardon		Knowl-edge	Confes-sion	I. John v. 4
" viii. 37, 38	Faith	......	Confes-sion	Baptism		......		Temper-ance	Prayer	Victory
" x. 48	......	......	Confes-sion	Baptism		......		Patience	Pardon	I. Cor. xv. 57
" xvi.15	......	......	......	Baptism		......		Godliness	Comfort of the Spirit	Crown
" xvi. 31, 33	Faith	......	......	Baptism		Saved		Brotherly kindness	I. John ii. 1	II. Tim. iv. 8
" xxii. 16	......	......	......	Baptism		Wash		Charity I. Pet. i. 5-8	I. John i. 9	......

Method: { Faith. Repent-ance. Confes-sion. Baptism. (Gal. iii. 27).

IN CHRIST,

ALL IS YEA AND AMEN. (II. Cor. i. 20.)

GLORY OF GOD. (Rom. xv. 7.)

L. D. McGowan,
Clarksburg, Ind.

XXVI.—ACTS OF THE APOSTLES.

[The apostles were to " begin " to " bear witness " " at (1) Jerusalem," and then go into (2) Judea, Samaria, and (3) to the uttermost part of the earth. The history of Acts shows that exactly this order was followed.]

IN EXPLAINING the diagram, but little need be said. The first circle represents what is recorded in Acts of the Apostles, i. to vii. Among the events are the Ascension, the Waiting, Pentecost, Stoning of Stephen, etc.

Circle two embraces the events recorded in Acts viii. to xiii.

Circle three, those recorded in chapters xiii. to xxi.

The last, or circle four, embraces events found in chapters xxi. to xxviii.

The apostles were to " begin " to bear witness " at Jerusalem," then go into " Judea and Samaria," and then " to the uttermost part of the earth." The history in Acts of Apostles shows that they followed exactly this order.

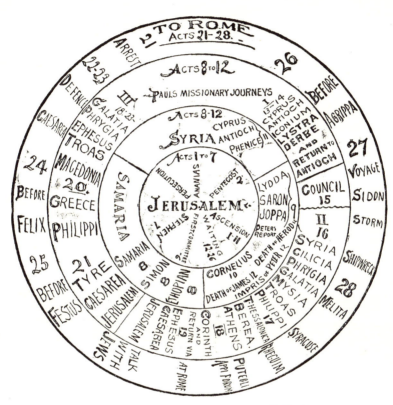

E. R. BLACK,
Buchanan, Mich.

XXVII.—New Testament or Apostolic Church.

TO THE right of the larger brace we have an outline of what the New Testament church consisted, with the admonition at the top to "make all things according to the pattern." This quotation by Paul, from the Book of Exodus, was God's oft-repeated command concerning the construction of the tabernacle in the wilderness, which was a type of the true church ; and if God was so particular in regard to the tabernacle, the type, how much more so of the organization of the church, the body of whom Christ is the head ? If God does not permit any addition to or subtraction from his Word, will he allow changes in the organization and government of his church not warranted in the Scriptures ? See reference in upper right-hand corner of chart.

Under the small brace, opposite the word FOUNDER at the top, we see that Christ was the builder of his own church, that it was built upon the foundation or by the authority of apostles and prophets, Jesus Christ being chief in all. That it was spiritual in character and composed of visible organized bodies of men and women, and that the law of conquest, expressed in the great commission, was to reach all nations, going into effect at Jerusalem on the first Pentecost after the resurrection of Jesus. The references should always be traced from left to right, in the order given, clear across the chart.

Under the next brace below we find that the organization consists of saints, elders and deacons. Under the small brace, opposite saints, we see they were called of God, how and for what purpose. Under the two small braces, opposite elders and deacons, we find the authority for the office of these officers, with their character and duty defined in the references cited, and the duty of the church to her officers.

In the next brace below we have the "NAME OF" ORGANIZATION and the individual MEMBERS, as given in the Scriptures and ENDORSED by the APOSTLES. The sinfulness of taking human names and the authority for taking the name Christian. Next come the ORDINANCES. Under the small brace, opposite baptism, the references show who are SCRIPTURAL subjects for baptism, how they were baptized, and what was its design.

Then comes the Lord's Supper, showing when and by whom instituted, its importance, when and how often to be observed, fixing the responsibility as to who should partake, and setting forth the penalty for partaking unworthily. Opposite the word DISCIPLINE, next in order, we find the Word of God alone was used, and was amply sufficient for church government.

Then the CREED of the apostolic church, the Christ, of what it consisted and how used. That it was unchangeable, adapted to all ages, needing no revision. The WORD of God is the seed of the kingdom, and without the SEED the FRUIT of the kingdom can not be produced. If all the religious people of the world were to renounce the creeds and doctrines of men and follow the simple New Testament pattern or model, the prayer of Jesus in the seventeenth chapter of John would be answered, the law of the Spirit in Rom. xvi. 17, 18; I. Cor. i. 10-13; iii. 1-4, 11, 16-18, obeyed, and all of God's people would be one. Thus united, the hosts of God would be thrown against the bulwarks of sin and the world converted to Christ instead of sects and parties. An unprejudiced appeal to this chart will show at once the fallacy of calling the people who are endeavoring to reproduce this divine order of church life and work "Campbellites," since this divine model was in existence at least seventeen centuries before Alexander Campbell was born, as shown by the Scriptures here cited. The kingdom of heaven was intended for all nations (Matt. xxix. 19), hence its platform must be broad enough for all people to accept. The Creed, Discipline, Ordinances, Name, Organization and Founder, are all union ground, and no one can reject either one without rejecting the Bible and its Author, the Author of salvation to that extent. This platform proves its divine origin, and the plea is divine. The primitive church preached their creed according to their discipline, and obeyed the ordinances as set forth therein, accepted only such names as given by divine authority, and organized their converts according to the law given by their FOUNDER.

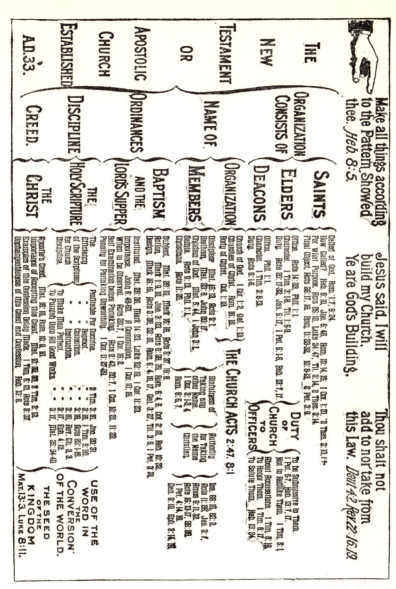

Make all things according to the Pattern showed thee. *Heb 8:5.*

Jesus said, I will build my Church, Ye are God's Building.

Thou shalt not add to nor take from this Law. *Deut 4:2 Rev 22:18,19*

THE NEW TESTAMENT OR APOSTOLIC CHURCH ESTABLISHED A.D. 33.

ORGANIZATION CONSISTS OF — SAINTS — ELDERS — DEACONS

NAME OF — ORGANIZATION — MEMBERS

THE CHURCH ACTS 2:47; 8:1

ORDINANCES — BAPTISM AND THE LORD'S SUPPER

DISCIPLINE — HOLY SCRIPTURE

CREED. — CHRIST THE

USE OF THE WORD IN THE CONVERSION OF THE WORLD.

THE SEED OF THE KINGDOM

Mat.13:3. Luke 8:11.

J. A. L. ROMIG.

XXVIII.—A FOUR-FOLD GOSPEL.

WHY four gospels? *Answer:* No man is large enough to take in Jesus Christ. "The gospel according to Matthew" means what Matthew apprehended of it. Likewise, "According to Mark," etc. As no man can give out what he does not receive, it clearly follows that no one man can reveal a full gospel.

Matthew was a tax-gatherer, accustomed to systematic statement, and we find his business habits running through his testimony. Notice his grouping of miracles in the eighth and ninth chapters, and the parables in the thirteenth, and the prophecies in the twenty-fourth and twenty-fifth. He alone gives, in completeness, the Sermon on the Mount; the discourse concerning John; the denunciation of the Scribes and Pharisees; the parables of the tares, hid treasure, pearl, draw-net, laborers in the vineyard, the talents and ten virgins.

Mark writes the "gospel of action." He omits all questions of genealogy and such things as would not interest his Roman readers. He describes the baptism of Christ in three verses, his temptation in two, and proceeds at once to his wonderful works. He distinctly describes three miracles in the first chapter, with the additional testimony that "he healed many that were sick of divers diseases, and cast out many devils."

Luke is more evangelical than either Mark or Matthew. He proclaims good tidings of great joy that shall be to all people. He gives us the parable of the good Samaritan and the prodigal son, both of which strike at race and caste prejudice. Matthew is content to make Jesus the son of David. Luke traces him back to Adam, and makes him stand for all mankind.

John writes what Clement calls the "gospel of spirit;" Ernesti, "the heart of Christ;" and Pressense, "the gospel of the idea." Augustine says: "While the three other evangelists remain below with the man, Christ Jesus, and speak but little of his Godhead, John, as if impatient of setting his foot on the earth, rises, from the very first words of his gospel, not only above earth and the span of air and sky, but above all angels and invisible powers, till he reaches Him by whom all things were made." "In the beginning was the Word, and the Word was with God."

A FOURFOLD GOSPEL

Mathew	Wrote to	Deals with	Records Mainly	Points to	Demonstrates
	Israel	Their past History	Discourses to the Multitudes	Kingdom of Heaven	Tha Jesus of Nazereth is the Son of David
Mark	Gentiles	The Present & Future	Christs Mighty Works.	Kingdom of Power	Son of Man
Luke	Both	Past Present Future	Parables & Miracles	Kingdom of Good Will	Son of Adam
John	Christians	Time & Eternity	Talks to those chosen to be Apostles	Kingdom of Spirits	Son of God
All Four	All Mankind	With all Human History	What Jesus was. said & did.	Kingdoms of Heaven Power Good Will Spirts	The Christ the Son. of the Living God.

XXIX.—WORLD'S FIVE GREAT EMPIRES

WE have in the Bible brief accounts of five great empires:

I. THE SUPERNAL.

That over which God directly rules in the Heaven of heavens. It embraces all the ranks of cherubim and seraphim, archangels and angels, and the law of their government is the will of God.

II. THE INFERNAL.

That over which Satan rules, and embracing all ranks of fallen angels who inhabit the hopeless land, and are entirely led captive at the will of the devil.

III. THE MEDIATORIAL.

That in which Christ is King, and all who believe in and try to obey him are subjects. Its territory is the earth, and the law of its government is the Word of God.

IV. PAPAL.

This represents the great apostasy over which anti-Christ holds sway on earth. It is governed by human authority, and has human ordinances, and practices customs not authorized by the Word of God.

V. THE ETERNAL.

That which will be the result of the merging of the mediatorial into the supernal. When Christ, having put all enemies under his feet, and destroyed the last enemy—death—shall deliver up the kingdom to God the Father, who shall be all in all, in that kingdom we shall be joint heirs with Christ himself.

FIVE GREAT EMPIRES.

WORLDS	KING,—	SUBJECTS.	TERRITORY.	LAWS.
SUPERNAL	GOD.	ARCHANGELS, ALL ANGELS, CHERUBIM, SERAPHIM	THE HEAVEN OR HEAVENS	GODS WILL
INFERNAL	SATAN.	ALL RANKS AND ORDERS OF FALLEN ANGELS.—	THE HOPELESS ABODE OF EVIL ONES	WILL OF the DEVIL
MEDIATORIAL	CHRIST—	ALL WHO BELIEVE IN HIM & OBEY HIM TO THE BEST OF THEIR ABILITY.	THIS EARTH	THE BIBLE
PAPAL."	POPES	ALL WHO PAY ALLEGIANCE TO The SUPREME PONTIFF	THE ROMANIST PART OF THIS WORLD	THE LAWS OF THE CHURCH & DECREES OF THE POPES & COUNCIL
ETERNAL.	GOD.	ALL UNFALLEN & REDEEMED ONES.	THE NEW JERUSALEM & CITY OF LIGHT & COUNCIL	LOVE

E. B. SCOFIELD.

XXX.—SALVATION A TYPE.

TEXT.—I. Cor. x. 1-11.

A STUDY of the types in the Old Testament is an important way in making clear the plan of salvation. The types seem to be of a three-fold character: (*a*) Historical, (*b*) Legal, (*c*) Prophetical. This study would be classified under the first head. Paul, in referring to the history of fleshly Israel, said: " All these things happened unto them for examples, and are written for our admonition upon whom the ends of the world are come " (I. Cor. x. 11).

The chart explains itself. The degrading bondage in Egypt is typical of the slavish bondage of sin. The mission of Moses to those Israelites was to be a savior, a deliverer, a leader. This is typical of Christ's mission to the world. Moses' mission was confirmed by miracles (Ex. vii.). Likewise Christ was confirmed by miracles (John ii. 23; iii. 2; vi. 14; vii. 31). Moses' mission having been confirmed, he was believed in and accepted. Likewise Christ. They were baptized unto Moses in the cloud and Red Sea (I. Cor. x. 2). So are we baptized into Christ (Gal. iii. 27). The law given at Sinai for the guidance of fleshly Israel is typical of the law of Zion for the guidance of spiritual Israel (Mic. iv. 2; Isa. ii. 3). The disciplines, trials and providences of the wilderness is prophetic of the disciplines, trials and providences of the Christian life. The Jordan is symbolical of death :

> "Even death's cold wave I will not flee,
> Since God through Jordan leadeth me."

The promised land is typical of our promised home.

SALVATION IN TYPE

TYPE	ANTITYPE
1 Bondage in Egypt	1 Bondage in Sin
2 Mission of Moses	2 Mission in Christ
3 The Miracles of Moses	3 Its Miracles of Christ
4 Moses Accepted	4 Christ Accepted
5 Baptized unto Moses	5 Baptized into Christ
6 Law of Moses (Mt Sinai)	6 Law of Christ
7 Wilderness Experience	7 Christian Life
8 Physical Food Given	8 Spiritual Food Given
9 Jordan	9 Death
10 Canaan	10 Heaven

AUSTIN HUNTER.

XXXI.—CHURCHES OF ASIA.

IN STUDYING the Epistles to the Seven Churches, we find—

1. Christ addresses to these churches words of (*a*) Commenda-tion, (*b*) Condemnation, (*c*) Exhortation, (*d*) Promise.

2. That Christ begins with commendation and ends with prom-ise.

3. There is something to commend in each church, but in two—Smyrna and Philadelphia—there is nothing to condemn.

4. The promises depend upon heeding the exhortations.

5. As the number seven is symbolical of universality, the Seven Churches stand for the Universal Church.

6. Therefore, all that is said to them comes with equal force to churches in like condition to-day.

LETTERS TO THE SEVEN CHURCHES.

LANGUAGE OF	COMMENDATION	CONDEMNATION	EXHORTATION	PROMISE V.7.
EPHESUS	GOOD WORKS V.2 / PATIENCE " / PURITY " / INTELLIGENCE " / PERSEVERENCE "3	DECLENSION V.4	REMEMBER V.5 / REPORT " / REFORM "	FRUITS OF TREE V.T. / IN PARADISE -
SMYRNA	WORKS / TRIBULATION / POVERTY / PERSECUTION		BE THOU FAITHFUL V.10 / " FEARLESS 10.	NOT BE HURT / OF THE SECOND / DEATH - V.11.
PERGAMOS	WORKS V.13 / ABODE NAME 13 / HOLD FAITH 13 / MARTYRDOM " 13	DOCTRINE OF BALAAM / " " NICOLAITANS	REPENT	HIDDEN MANNA / WHITE STONE / NEW NAME V.17
THYATIRA	WORKS CHARITY / SERVICE FAITH / PATIENCE & WORKS / V.19	JEZEBEL	HOLD FAST / WHAT YOU HAVE	POWER OVER NATIONS V.26 / MORNING STAR V.28
SARDIS	WORKS - V.1 / PURITY "	NAME WITHOUT LIFE - V.1 / IMPERFECTION - V.2	BE WATCHFUL V.2 / REMEMBER V.3 / HOLDFAST V.3	WHITE RAIMENT-V.5 / NAME WRITTEN INV.5. / BOOK / CONFESSED V.5.
PHILADELPHIA	STRENGTH V.8 / KEPT WORD " / " NAME " "		HOLDFAST V.11.	KEEP FROM TEMPTA-TION. V.10 / PILLAR IN TEMPLE
LAODICEA		LUKEWARMNESS - V.16 / EGOTISM " 17 / & POVERTY " 17	"BUY GOLD V.18 / WHITE RAIMENT" 11 / BE ZEALOUS & " 19 / REPENT	SIT DOWN ON / THRONE V.21 / SUP WITH " 20 / CHRIST " 20

XXXII.—Seven Steps in the Humiliation of Christ.

INTRODUCTION.—Every step in the humiliation of Christ is contrary to the desire or nature of man. Man's desire is to elevate self; he strives in life to rise in prominence before his fellow man.

First step. Divested of all former glory, left the glory of a prince. Man striving for position, political and educational.

Second. He descends. Man's desire to climb.

Third. Takes upon himself the form of sinful man—flesh, blood and bone. No one could look upon God and live (Jno. iv. 24). Moses at the burning bush. That the love of God might be manifest, he took on the form of humanity.

Fourth. Makes himself of no reputation. He goes to the poverty of the world, not kings and queens. Man does the opposite.

Fifth. Our nature, our sufferings—the ailments of life.

Sixth. Position of a servant; as an act of humiliation, washes the disciples' feet (Jno. xiii. 8–15). He came to serve.

Seventh. Isa. liii. 7, 8: Humbles himself and became obedient unto death; he was led as a lamb to the slaughter; in his humiliation his judgment taken away; speechless and dumb, his humiliation reaches below man's.

Conclusion. I. Pet. v. 6: God exalts those who humble themselves in his sight. He will exalt you in due time if you exalt him now. This is done by a life of humiliation and sacrifice.

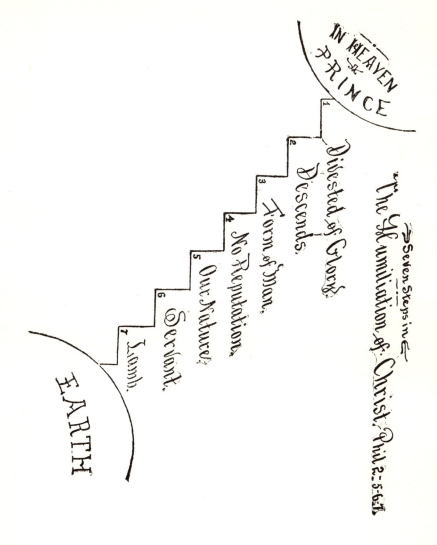

IN HEAVEN
&
PRINCE

The Humiliation of Christ. Phil. 2:-5-6-7.

⇒ Seven Steps in ⇐

1 Divested of Glory
2 Descends.
3 Form of Man.
4 No Reputation.
5 Our Nature.
6 Servant.
7 Lamb.

EARTH

XXXIII.—TEXT : II. Tim. i. 13.

THE term *form* in this text is very important. In the universe there are two great volumes: (1) The Book of Nature ; (2) The Bible. Both of these had one author ; both were made, and hence both had a beginning. Doubtless what are called the original elements in nature had a beginning. The primordial atoms of matter have definite shape, size and such characteristics as indicate *reason* and *design*, proving beyond a doubt that they were manufactured and were the creation or product of mind. To prove the beginning of matter, we present the following axioms: (1) " Nothing can not produce something." (2) " Something now exists ; hence, something has always existed." (3) " That which always existed had no beginning." (4) " That which had no beginning must be absolutely and eternaly independent." (5) " Matter is not independent, and hence it was created."

2. The Bible was also *made*. Reason teaches that if God created man, he would seek to govern him ; and hence he must speak to man. The will of God is found in the Bible.

3. God does not *formulate* in either of these books.

4. These two volumes, having the same infallible Author, must be in strict harmony. The Bible is a verbal revelation of the power, wisdom and goodness of God ; the Book of Nature is a pictorial revelation of the same attributes of God. The Bible is on a higher plane ; it meets the demands of man's moral and spiritual nature. The Book of Nature feeds the intellect ; the Bible feeds the spiritual nature of man.

5. The entire volume of nature is composed of a few simple or elementary substances ; so the Bible has few simple or basic elements. In the volume of nature there are some sixty-seven simple elements known to exist ; so in the Bible there are but twenty-six simple elements, called letters in English, twenty-five in Latin and twenty-four in Greek. Everything we see in nature is a composition or a combination of different simple elements, as earth, air, fire, water, etc. So all the words in the Bible, with but three exceptions, viz., A, I and O, are a combination of letters. The sixty-seven simple or elementary substances, in combination make up the entire material world—a ponderous volume truly. So in combination the twenty-six letters make up all the myriads of books and papers published in the English language.

6. In nature God combined these elements as only they could be combined, so as to reach or secure the results desired. The form and proportion of these elements, in combination, is an essential matter. Let us illustrate by water, which is composed of two parts of hydrogen in volume and one part of oxygen, or eight parts of oxygen in weight, and one part of hydrogen. No other proportion of these elements, in combination, will constitute water. Notice, also, common air, the very *pabulum* of life, is composed of four parts of nitrogen and one part of oxygen, mixed, but not chemically combined. If these proportions changed, men must die. What an exquisite adaptation to man and animals, and yet some contend that there is no intelligent Creator ! Let us now notice six different combinations of oxygen and nitrogen :

NITROGEN.	OXYGEN.	
N^4O......4 parts	1 part	......Air.
N^2O......2 "	1 "	......Laughing Gas.
$N O$......1 "	1 "	......Nitric Oxide.
N^2O^3......2 "	3 parts	......Nitrous Anhydride.
$N O^2$......1 "	2 "	......Nitrogen Peroxide.
N^2O^5......2 "	5 "	......Nitric Anhydride.

All these, except air, are deadly to man. So God combined letters and words so as to make the Bible (II. Tim. i. 13). A different arrangement of the twenty-six letters will make the Bible and " The Age of Reason." The *arrangement*, or *form*, makes the difference. To change the form of sound words is to change the gospel of Christ. We must take God's form of words in the gospel as we must take God's combination of oxygen and nitrogen in common air.

1. The form of words and the gospel may be changed by addition. Thus *one* becomes *none*, and *here* becomes *there*. In an article written for publication, a young physician spoke of " Caries of the bones," but the compositor added two letters, making " Carries off the bones ! "

2. The form may be changed by subtraction. Thus *shoe* becomes *hoe* and *danger* becomes *anger*. A lady compositor omitted c in the sentence, " We shall all be changed " (I. Cor. xv. 51).

3. The form changed by changing the arrangement of the elements. Thus *Levi, veil, live, evil*. A little girl in Sunday-school, who was offered a prize on condition she would recite from memory the first chapter of James correctly, failed on the twelfth verse. She said. "And when he is *tired*, he shall receive a crown of life."

4. The form changed by substitution. Thus a *fan* becomes a *man*, and a *fig* becomes a *pig*. In an article prepared for publication, the author spoke of "The devil's work," but the printer substituted *p* for *w*, making it "devil's pork." The following sentence was found some time since in the Chicago *News*, "All *wives* should be put under the ground," *v* being substituted for *r*. In a Massachusetts paper, not long since, in a eulogistic notice of a deceased lawyer, the reporter wished to say, "The body was taken to Hull for interment, where reposed the remains of other members of the family," but the printer substituted *e* for *u* in Hull!

Referring to the diagram, note the prerequisites of each step into the church of Christ. To the condition of salvation we must not add, from them we must not subtract; we must not change God's arrangement of them; we must not substitute anything for any of them. We must take and hold fast the form of sound words.

In the church, with faith, hope and love, we must live soberly, righteously and godly, and thus seek for glory, honor and immortality. Notice the everlasting kingdom of God beyond death and the resurrection. Here God, Christ, angels and glorified saints, invested with the crown of life eternal, will dwell forever.

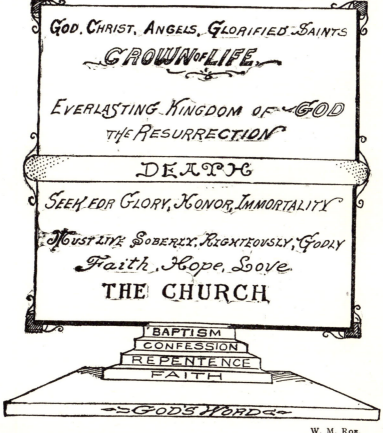

W. M. Rox.

XXXIV.—ALLEGORY OF SARAH AND HAGAR.

TEXT.—Gal. iv. 22-31.

IN ANSWER to the question, "In the light of this allegory, what lesson is deducible from the difference between the births of the two sons and from the consequent casting out of Hagar and Ishmael from all prospect of inheritance?" the Exegetical Analysis presents the following:

"Those who suppose that the church of the New Testament had its organic beginning in the family of Abraham, and simply realized its completeness after the coming of Christ, would do well to study the lessons of this allegory.

"That the gospel, in the form of unexplained and unfulfilled promise of spiritual blessing through his seed, was announced to Abraham, has already been seen from Gal. iii. 8 and its context. It is there made clear that this promise of undefined spiritual blessing only vaguely embodied '*the faith which should afterwards be revealed.*' Now, the supposition that on the basis of this unexplained promise, whose spiritual contents remained to be '*afterwards revealed*' in and through Christ, a 'spiritual society' was organized in the family of Abraham, constituting what Calvin calls a '*vera ecclesia,*' is not only a fiction of modern theology, but is palpably at variance with Paul's teaching in the allegory before us. Let it be carefully noted that while Isaac, as the child of promise, and born unto freedom, allegorically represented the future spiritual seed of Abraham as children by faith and heirs through Christ of the spiritual inheritance (iii. 29), it was, nevertheless, through Isaac himself that the kind of posterity came which Ishmael allegorically represented—*the offspring of Abraham according to the flesh,* and hence debarred, as such, from all inheritance *in the spiritual sense* of the promise. Isaac, as the son of Sarah, became heir of the temporal inheritance from which Ishmael, as the son of Hagar, the bondwoman, was actually excluded, and this exclusion, according to Paul's understanding, represented the exclusion of Isaac's descendants, or Abraham's natural posterity through Isaac, from all participation, as mere descendants of his, from the spiritual inheritance to be obtained through Christ. Thus all of Isaac's descendants, the whole Jewish people, as subsequently organized under the legal covenant at Sinai, were subjects of that covenant which bore 'children unto bondage,' and so were 'kept in ward under the law,' shut up unto the faith which was afterwards to be revealed on the coming of Christ. Who now were left in Abraham's family to be organized into a 'Gospel Church,' on the basis of an undefined promise of something not even revealed under that dispensation? All Jews stood in covenant relation with the God of Abraham, simply because they were 'born after the flesh,' as the patriarch's offspring by nature, and all those carnal institutions, like circumcision, which were connected with his history, belong, by their very nature, not to the spiritual side of the promise, which found fulfillment only in the Messianic Kingdom, but to the eternal side alone, and were ultimately embraced in the national covenant at Mt. Sinai. Hence, Jesus speaks of circumcision as an element of the law of Moses (John vii. 23).

"Now, 'what say the Scriptures? Cast out the handmaid and her son: for the son of the handmaid shall not inherit with the son of the freewoman.' As interpreted by Paul, abrogate the Old Covenant with its carnal provisions, and set aside its subjects who, as 'born after the flesh,' shall not inherit with the spiritual children of the New Covenant, who are heirs through Christ on the principle of faith. Those, therefore, who now claim to be 'really and truly born citizens of the visible commonwealth of Christ, as they are born citizens of the commonwealth of the United States or of Great Britain' (*Stuart Robinson,* in 'Discourses of Redemption,' page 86), virtually abandon Christianity for Judaism, or blindly blend together two incompatible administrations. By the clear provisions of the New Covenant itself, which was typified by Sarah, and predicted as still in the future by Jeremiah, though indefinitely embodied in the promise to Abraham on its spiritual side, the principle of flesh with its consequence of infant membership, is distinctly repudiated as having no place in the church of the New Testament. ' Behold, the days come, says the Lord, that I will make a new covenant with the house of Israel and the house of Judah. Not according to the covenant I made with their fathers in the day that I took them by the hand to lead them forth out of the land of Egypt. For this is the covenant that I will make with the house of Israel after those days, says the Lord; I will put my laws into their mind, and on their heart also will I write them: And I will be to them a God, and they shall be to me a people: And they shall not teach every man his fellow citizen, and every man his brother, saying, Know the Lord; For all shall know me, from the least to the greatest of them' (Heb. viii. 8-12; Jer. xxxi. 31-34).

"Now, even supposing the 'gospel church,' or Messiah's Kingdom, to have had its beginning under the Old Testament, we have here a new constitution, with new provisions of citizenship, in accordance with which none shall be citizens who are *too little* to *know the Lord,* as having come in by natural birth, but must enter as having the laws of God 'put into their mind' and 'written upon their heart,' and are thus able to 'know the Lord, from the least to the greatest of them.' "

"We add that innocent babes can, through the Redeemer's reversal of the Adamic overthow, enter the kingdom above without the instrumentality of a covenant or church" (Rom. v. 15-19).

DIAGRAM PRESENTING THE TWELVE ANALOGIES AND TWELVE ANTITHESES OF THE LAW AND THE GOSPEL IN ALLEGORY (Gal. iv. 21, 31).

(a) **Mothers**	THE HANDMAID VS. THE FREEWOMAN.	THE OLD COVENANT 24 VS. THE NEW COVENANT. 26, 31
(b) **Sons**	ISHMAEL VS. ISAAC.	JEWS UNDER THE OLD VS. CHRISTIANS UNDER THE NEW.
(c) **Births**	BY NATURE AS TO ISHMAEL VS. THROUGH PROMISE AS TO ISAAC	NATURAL BIRTH OF THE SUBJECTS OF THE OLD 29 VS. SPIRITUAL BIRTH OF THE SUBJECTS OF THE NEW. 28
(d) **Dispositions**	ISHMAEL A PERSECUTOR VS. ISAAC'S ENDURANCE.	JEWISH PERSECUTIONS 29 VS. CHRISTIAN ENDURANCE.
(e) **States**	DOMESTIC BONDAGE AS TO ISHMAEL VS. DOMESTIC FREEDOM AS TO ISAAC.	LEGAL BONDAGE 25 OF THE JEWS VS. SPIRITUAL LIBERTY 31 OF CHRISTIANS.
(f) **Results**	ISHMAEL CAST OUT VS. ISAAC MADE HEIR.	REJECTION OF JEWS 30 VS. ACCEPTANCE OF CHRISTIANS. 30

PROF. I. B. GRUBBS.

XXXV.—DISPENSATION OF RELIGION.

THE diagram is intended to show the special design of the dispensations: Patriarchal, Mosaic and Christian. The first began B. C. 4004 and ended B. C. 1500. The second began B. C. 1500 and ended A. D. 33. The third began A. D. 33 and will end with time. The special objects of these dispensations were to illustrate respectively three fundamental principles of religion, viz.: The Being of God, the Atonement and Immortality.

In the Patriarchal dispensation we see a remarkable manifestation of the presence and being of God. He walks with man and talks with him face to face. There is also a hint at the atonement in the sacrifice of Abel, and of immortality in the translation of Enoch.

The special design of the Mosaic dispensation was to illustrate the idea of atonement. To this end were all its sacrifices and offerings. There is also a hint at the being of God in the Shechinah, and of the doctrine of immortality in the translation of Elijah.

The special design of the Christian dispensation is to illustrate the doctrine of man's immortality. But it also shows a glimpse of the being of God at the death of Stephen, and the atonement in the Lord's Supper.

That God is, that he is approached through sacrifice, and that man is immortal, have always been the fundamental principles of all religion. That there has been a dispensation devoted primarily to each one of these fundamentals is sought to be shown by this diagram.

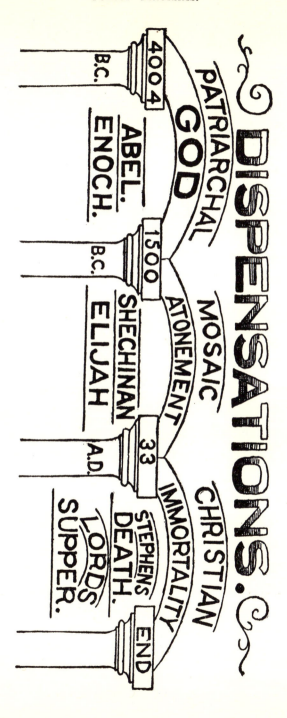

XXXVI.—POWER FOR SERVICE.

Power for Service.

Acts I 8.

Int Rem Kingdom based on Love not on Force

Three Spheres (a) Divine (b) Human = (c) Worlds Need

(Circle 1:) THE EARTH LIFE ENDED WITH THE ASCENSION — LIFE AND POWER IN Jesus — MATT 28 18 20

(Circle 2:) THE CHRIST LIFE CONVEYED INTO HUMAN SOULS — POWER FOR Service FROM SPIRIT — LU. 24 49 ACTS 1. 8

(Circle 3:) CHRIST IN YOU THE HOPE OF GLORY COL 2 27 — CHRIST IN MEN IS Salvation — EPH 3 17 GAL 2 20

Remarks 1 God is the only | Source of Life
2 Man is the only | Life Conveyer
3 Spirit-filled men | Proclaim Spirit given message
Power | Embraces.

As in beginning   the Apostles needed
1 Remembrance John 14. 26.
2 Guidance   John 16. 7 13
3 Utterance Acts 2 4 Eph 5 18-20
4 Assurance 1 Thess 1:4 5. Heb 2:3, 4.
5 Acceptance Acts 5: 32 Rom 5 6.

So now, We need -

1 Remembrance of memoirs of Jesus,
2 Guidance unto knowledge of all Revealed Truth
3 Utterance of Word in living tongues.
4 Asurance by "Signs Written and Experiences
5 Acceptance with hearers 1 Cor 13 Eph 4.15
So Spirits presence is prerequisite to Evangelism

Promise in Matt 28·20.

W. L. HAYDEN.

XXXVII.—THE TRINITIES OF CHRISTIANITY.

TEXT.—I. Cor. xv. 1-4.

THE essential elements of the Christian religion are all presented to us in the Scriptures as a series of trinities; a succession of groups, each made up of three constituents, and each
three composing a unit of higher order. This is an interesting and
instructive fact—capable, when duly considered, of guiding us to
a clearer and fuller comprehension of the whole scheme of redemption. It is not, however, an exceptional fact, nor one the existence of which should at all surprise us. We are accustomed to
the perception and recognition of trinities in everything; in the
world, as made up of three kingdoms—the mineral, the vegetable
and the animal; in matter, as exhibited under three forms—solid,
fluid and gaseous; in our own being, as body, soul and spirit; and
even in the Creator himself, whose works reveal him, to reverent
observation and reflection, as a Being of goodness, wisdom and
power—attributes which are themselves adequately described only
by the three qualifying attributes—infinite, immutable and eternal.
When, therefore, this great Being comes to make a clearer revelation of himself in his word—the fact that he presents himself
to the apprehension of our faith as Father, Son and Holy Spirit—
should not be a matter of surprise to our reason, nor of difficulty
to our belief.

If, then, in Nature itself; in the revelations made by Nature,
and in the higher doctrine of the Word, we everywhere find three
in one, or three making one, we are prepared to expect the same
thing in the gospel and its concomitants; and are pleased and edi-
fied rather than surprised to discover that all the essential elements
of Christian doctrine are exhibited in a succession of trinities.

Let us consider each of these trinities in the order presented
on the Chart.

Having now reached the end of this most suggestive and instructive series of trinities, we look back for a moment to note one very
remarkable fact connected with them. It is this: That while in
each of these threes the first and second elements have a distinct
importance and value of their own, *the realization of this value*

to us is dependent upon the third constituent of the trinity. This
will be so obvious, after a moment's consideration, that very little
time need be occupied in illustrating it.   Let us look, for instance,
at the three essential attributes of God, as exhibited in his works.
It is obvious that it was his *goodness* which prompted the creation
of worlds, and of beings capable of happiness; that it was his
wisdom that devised how this was to be done; but it was the third
attribute, *power*, which *actualized* these promptings of goodness,
and these counsels of wisdom, and brought them forth as cog-
nizable facts.

In like manner it may be said that no words can express the
comfort and bliss of knowing this great Being as our *Father*, or of
knowing that our Elder Brother, the Lord Jesus Christ, is the
veritable *Son* of the Father.   But we are dependent for this knowledge upon the third, the *Holy Spirit*, who alone *reveals* to us the
Father and the Son.   And with reference to this Son, every one
will instantly perceive the inadequacy of his *prophetic* and *priestly*
offices to accomplish their own purpose in human salvation, separate
and apart from his *kingly* dignity and power.   He must reign and
rule in the midst of his enemies.

If now we glance at the distinctive elements of the gospel, which
it has been mainly the purpose to illustrate, the same fact will
appear.   He died for our sins, and was buried.   Stupendous facts
—precious beyond all conception !   But what are they to us without the third, the completion of the trinity ?   " If Christ be not
risen, your faith is *vain;* ye are yet in your sins."   True, it was
the first fact of the gospel—the shedding of blood—that takes
away sins ; but, mark you, the efficacy of that blood is dependent
upon his resurrection.   For, if he be not risen, he is not the Son
of God, and his sacrifice is *vain*, and the faith that rests upon it
is vain.

It is hardly necessary to remark that the same law obtains respecting the three acts—faith, repentance and baptism, which constitute the Scriptural acceptance of the gospel.   The first and second
have their own essential value, but this value, for the purpose now
in view, is suspended and conditioned upon the third.

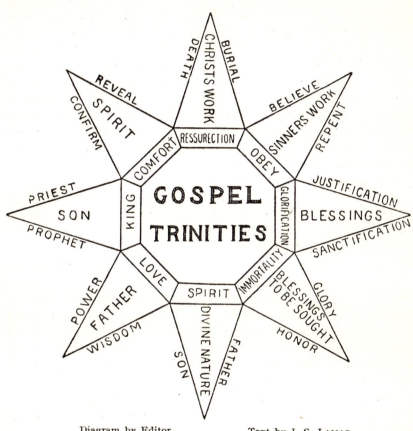

Diagram by Editor.   Text by J. S. LAMAR.

XXXVIII.—THE OBELISKS OF GREAT BRITAIN.

EGYPT has long been famed for her monumental obelisks, which
have excited the astonishment and admiration of the ages.
These shapely columns, carved out of a single stone, rising in
front of her temples, in some instances not less than 127 feet high,
were but a part and portion of those countless Egyptian sculptures
which are unparalleled in all the history of human architecture.

Not less than seven different times has Egypt been ravaged by
conquering armies; and for generations she has been supplying the
museums of the world with mummies, idols and obelisks, and yet
it is said the little narrow valley of the Nile still contains more
sculptures than all the globe besides.

The obelisks of Egypt are scattered over the world. In Con-
stantinople, in Rome, in London, in Paris, in Berlin, in Florence,
in New York, and elsewhere, may be found these monuments of
ancient Egyptian art, some of which were, doubtless, like the pyramids, erected by tyrants who could command the resources of a
multitude of helpless subjects, and so built whatever they pleased,
regardless of labor or expense.

Christendom has her obelisks, built up for tyrants by an op-
pressed race, at the expense of tedious toil and endless labor; con-
suming the time, the strength, the earnings and the lives of the
people. For the different obelisks may fitly represent the outlay
of the working men of Great Britain, and the objects for which
they expend their money—the most imposing of all representing
the outlay for strong drink. The nation's expense for food, rai-
ment, education, etc., seems light and moderate, while the outlay
for Christian missions appears positively insignificant in comparison
with the hideous total expended for base indulgence in intoxicating
beverages.

There are abundant facts and estimates to indicate the magni-
tude of the nation's outlay for this blighting curse. As a specimen,
we quote the following from "Facts and Figures on the Temperance
Question," by Rev. A. R. Wallace, of Toronto:

"The extent and expense of the liquor traffic in Great Britain,
the United States and Canada, is enormous. About one-seventh
of the grain of Great Britain is wasted on this traffic, when thousands of the people are on the verge of starvation, and living in
abject poverty. In the United Kingdom 52,659,000 bushels of

grain are destroyed yearly to make beer. One hundred million bushels of grain are annually destroyed in the Anglo-Saxon world, which would give two barrels of flour to every family in England, the United States and Canada during the year.

"During the last seven years, the large total has been spent of £987,000,000, or £200,000,000 more than the national debt of Great Britain. And this was not all, for it cost at least £100,000,000 more to pay for the mischief that it caused. That gave a cost of £241,000,000 yearly for their drink bill! It is said that there are about 200,000 places in Great Britain where liquor is sold, and these are probably doing more to hinder God's cause than the 40,000 ministers of religion can do to advance it.

"As the result, mainly of intemperance, they have nearly 3,000,-000 applying yearly for parish relief in that wealthy country; 85,000 inmates in their asylums; 60,000 convicted of crime; at least 250,000 vagrants roaming about the country; and about 120,000 brought annually to a premature grave. And these liquor shops are sanctioned by law to lead away the people from God, from happiness and heaven.

"Thus the liquor traffic of Great Britain costs as much as would support 600,000 missionaries at £240 a year; 500,000 schoolmasters at £100; build 5,000 churches at £2,000; 5,000 schoolhouses at £800; would give to the world 200,000,000 of Bibles at 1s. each; 500,000 of tracts at 4s. per hundred; would give 100,000 widows £20 a year; and 200,000 poor families £10 a year. In short, it would provide a machinery that would evangelize the world in a short time, or pay off the national debt in four years.

"In the United States there are 175,000 places where intoxicating liquor is sold, involving a direct outlay and waste of not less than £140,000,000; and an indirect loss to the country, by crime, pauperism, etc., of £140,000,000 more; and this results in the destruction of 100,000 lives yearly.

"In 1881 there were in operation in the United States 3,210 distilleries. These consumed 31,291,130 bushels of grain, with an aggregate production of 117,728,150 gallons of proof spirits. For the fiscal year ending June 30, 1881, the total amount of revenue to the national treasury from distilled spirits was £13,430,795; for the same period the total revenue from fermented liquors amounted to £2,740,049.

"The beer production for the year ending June 30, 1881, was 14,311,028 bushels, or, at thirty-one gallons per bushel, the enormous aggregate of 434,641,868 gallons.

"A brewer's authority gives the number of breweries at 2,830, and estimates that there are 1,681,670 acres of land under cultivation for barley and hops. If sown with wheat, at thirty bushels per acre, this land would provide 50,456,000 bushels, or about one bushel for every man, woman and child in the United States.

"It has been declared on authority of an official census, that the liquor traffic during the last ten years has sent 100,000 children to the poor-houses in the United States; has committed at least 150,-000 to prisons and workhouses; has made at least 10,000 insane; has determined at least 2,000 suicides; has caused the loss by fire or violence of £2,000,000 worth of property; and has made at least 200,000 widows and 1,000,000 orphans. While the clergymen of the United States cost £2,400,000 yearly, the loss to the nation, directly and indirectly, through liquor, is something like £280,000,-000 a year. The quantity of spirits and malt liquor made or imported into the Dominion of Canada, in 1882, was 17,733,934 gallons, or nearly four gallons for every man, woman and child in the Dominion. The liquor traffic is estimated to cost Canada £8,700,000 annually."

Egypt's pyramids and obelisks were prophecies of national ruin. The tyranny of rulers and degradation of subjects which alone made their erection possible, presaged the overthrow of that proud nation, which had for so many centuries been "the basest of kingdoms"; and such obelisks as those erected by modern European nations give solemn intimation of the overthrow and downfall of other kingdoms and empires through the tyranny of lust and vice.

Let us be warned in season. The firmer the obelisk, the more insecure the throne; the more majestic the monumental sculptures of the tyrants, the more squalid the homes of the people, and more debased the lives of the subjects who erect them.

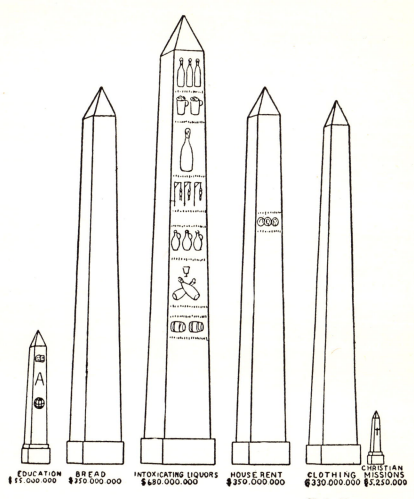

EDUCATION | BREAD | INTOXICATING LIQUORS | HOUSE RENT | CLOTHING | CHRISTIAN MISSIONS
$55.000.000 | $350.000.000 | $680.000.000 | $350.000.000 | $330.000.000 | $5.250.000

H. L. Hastings.

[FROM MISSIONARY TIDINGS, BY PERMISSION.]

XXXIX.—THE GREAT TEXT-BOOK.

1. The greatest book in the world.
   - (1) Its Divine origin. II. Peter i. 21.
   - (2) Its marvelous preservation from
       - (a) Pagan destruction.
       - (b) Papal suppression.
       - (c) Rationalistic criticism.
   - (3) The profound import of its message.
       - (a) Human sin.
       - (b) Divine love.
       - (c) The work of Christ. The expression of Divine Love in human terms. The ideal of a redeemed human nature.
   - Never was it so potent a force in society as to-day.

2. The most comprehensive book in the world. All rivers of thought flow into it, and from it come the influences that fashion all human endeavors.
   - (1) History. The only authentic history of the early ages is found in the Bible, and its history of the Chosen People, with its records of sin and punishment, is the prophecy of all future history. While it is not a historical text-book, it is yet the record of the most wonderful of all histories, that of Divine Revelation.
   - (2) Law. It is not a book of laws, and yet it contains the basis for the world's greatest codes, such as the Justinian, the Code Napoleon, and English and American civil law.
   - (3) Statesmanship. It has been the inspiration of the greatest statesmen of history, such as Gambetta, Lincoln and Gladstone, and its spirit has taught the world to abhor such crimes as the crushing of Hungary, the dismemberment of Poland, and the oppression of Ireland.
   - (4) Literature. The Bible is the fountain from which the foremost writers of the world have drawn their inspiration. Goethe, Hugo, Shakespeare, Scott, Dickens, Carlyle, Hawthorne, Emerson, and a host of others, have felt and acknowledged their indebtedness to this book. The best literature of all the years since it appeared has been saturated with its tone and spirit.

3. The most attractive book in the world.
   - (1) Its Literature—
       - (a) Poetry : The Psalms of Job. Canticles.
       - (b) Oratory : Judah's plea. The Orations and Sermons of the Prophets.
       - (c) Elegies: David's Song of the Bow.
       - (d) Hymns : Songs of Hannah, Zacharias, Mary and Simeon.
       - (e) Epistles : The letters of the New Testament, personal, doctrinal, apologetic, hortatory.
       - (f) Prophecy : Marvelous imagery. Majestic style. Profound import. Messianic tone.
   - (2) Its Narratives—
       - (a) Historical incidents of the Old Testament and New. The most charming and helpful stories of all literature.
       - (b) Character sketches : The lives of its heroes — Abraham, Joseph, David, Isaiah, Daniel, Paul, John. The world's greatest record of heroism.
       - (c) The Life of Jesus. "The most beautiful incarnation of God, in the most beautiful of forms."

4. The most influential book in the world. The effect of its teachings upon—
   - (1) The condition of woman.
   - (2) Childhood.
   - (3) Cruel sports, such as those of the Coliseum.
   - (4) War for plunder.
   - (5) Torture and cruel punishments.
   - (6) Human slavery.
   - (7) Intemperance and the crime of drunkard making.
   - (8) Unjust social relations.

H. L. WILLETT.

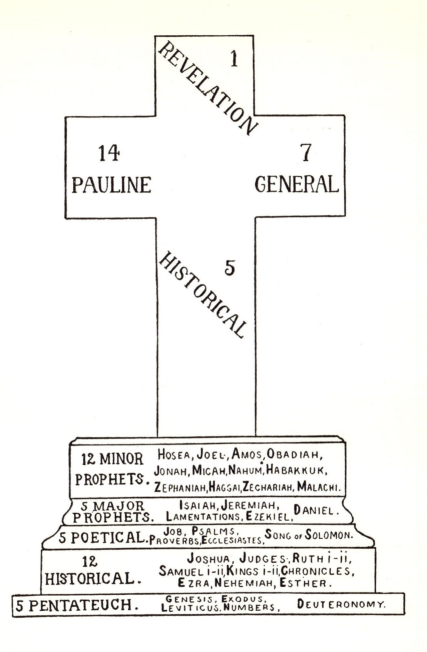

XLI.—CHRISTIAN UNITY.

COMMON GROUND.		SECTARIAN.
There is one true and living God, Creator of heaven and earth.	**God.**	Who is "without body or parts."
There is one Lord Jesus Christ, Son of God, and Saviour of sinners.	**Christ.**	"The very and eternal God." "Eternally begotten."
There is one Holy Spirit, who revealed divine truth, inspired men, convicts sinners, and comforts Christians.	**Holy Spirit.**	"Very and eternal God."
The Holy Scriptures are inspired of God, and are our only infallible rule of faith and practice.	**Rule of Faith and Practice.**	Other rules of faith and practice are also necessary to thoroughly furnish us.
Everything enjoined upon the people of the Christian dispensation by Christ or his apostles is of binding authority now.	**Of Binding Authority.**	Also, laws and commandments of the Jewish dispensation. Some of Christ's commands are non-essential.
1. The Holy Spirit operates on sinners in and through the gospel. 2. He dwells in Christians as their Comforter and Sanctifier.	**Operation of the Spirit.**	He also operates on sinners independently of the gospel. He also makes revelations to Christians now.
Whoever hears, believes and obeys the gospel with all the heart, is saved. "The gospel is the power of God unto salvation," etc.	**Salvation.**	Persons are also saved by the Holy Spirit independently of the gospel.
The truly penitent believer is a proper subject of Christian baptism.	**Subject of Baptism.**	Infants are also proper subjects.
The proper immersion in water of a penitent believer is valid Christian baptism.	**Action of Baptism.**	So also is the sprinkling or pouring of water upon an infant or penitent believer.
The baptized penitent believer stands forgiven of his past sins.	**Pardon.**	But he is pardoned before baptism, and the infant at baptism.
"The Church," the "Church of God," the "Kingdom of Heaven," the "Body of Christ," are Scriptural names for (of) the Church of Christ.	**Church Name.**	Methodist, Baptist, Presbyterian. etc., are proper names for "Branches of the Church."
The pardoned person is a child of God, is in Christ, is a member of the Church.	**Membership.**	Something else should be required of such before they are received into full fellowship.
All Christians who love God and the Lord Jesus, and who obey them faithfully to the end of life, will be saved in heaven.	**Ultimate Salvation.**	The wicked who die in their sins will finally be saved in heaven also.

M. INGELS.

REMARKS.

From the above presentation the reader will observe—

1. That the Disciples of Christ are pre-eminently an "orthodox" people, and that they plead for the union of God's people upon "the foundation of apostles and prophets, Jesus Christ himself being the chief corner–stone."

2. That on all questions of difference between the Disciples and any other Christian people, the Disciples must necessarily be on the *negative*, since *they* occupy the undisputed ground.

Permit an illustration :

Take the above item on the "action of baptism," for instance.

A discussion is pending on that question. What must the Disciple affirm? That a person may be validly baptized by immersion? No, this is already *admitted*. Hence, there could be no discussion on "immersion." But the Disciples do *deny* that a person can receive valid Christian baptism by sprinkling or pouring, because this is not "common," "orthodox," Scriptural ground, but "sectarian."

Thus every item above might be passed in review with the same results, viz.: All other evangelical churches would *agree* with the Disciples in every particular, and the Disciples would disagree with them only so far as the other churches are sectarian.

Every one should affirm only what he believes. He should never affirm a n gative, or an "only."

Dear reader, do you not desire to co-operate with that people who are laboring for the union of all of God's people in "one fold," having "one Shepherd"? May we all be led continually by the Spirit and counsel of the Lord, that we may finally enter upon everlasting joys at his right hand, where there are pleasures forevermore. "In *faith*, unity ; in *opinions*, liberty ; in *all things*, charity."

M. INGELS.

XLII.—THREE GARDENS.

GEN. II. 15; JOHN XIX. 41; REV. II. 7.

The sages say—

1. That happiness is the end of human existence.
2. That nature is a sufficient source of happiness.
3. That man's chief happiness is in forbidden objects.
4. That God is only what fancy makes him.
   But—
1. Happiness is not the end of human existence, but purity.
2. Nature is not the source of happiness, but God.
3. Man's chief happiness is not in forbidden objects, but in obedience to God's will.
4. Fancy is not the author of our Creator, nor our God what fancy makes him, but what revelation reveals him to be.

There are three things necessary for man's happiness—a religion, a companion, and a home; a family religion (and that would be universal), a Christian companion, and a happy home.

The gardens represent three momentous things—Life, Death, Destiny.

Destiny which comes to us from the death of Jesus in the life of communion with God.

(1)

In the first garden there is man as dresser of the garden; in the second, God dressed as man, yet free from sin; in the third, the saints dressed in the righteousness of Jesus.

(2)

1. Complete Life—mental, moral, physical.
2. Complete Death—in the physical only.
3. Complete Immortality—mental, moral, physical.

(3)

1. There was disobedience, and disobedience brought death.
2. There was obedience, and obedience brought life.
3. There is reward of obedience, and abundant entrance into eternal glory.

(4)

1. We enter the first garden with pleasure; we leave it with disgust.

2. We enter the second with disgust; we leave it with pleasure.

3. We enter the third to abide with joys unspeakable and full of glory.

(5)

1. There is the tree of life—forfeited.
2. There is the tree of life—regained.
3. There is the tree of life—enjoyed.

(6)

1. There is a dead soul (in sin).
2. There is a dead body.
3. There is the reunion of body and soul.

(7)

1. There is the fall, with its disasters.
2. There is the restoration, with its blessings.
3. There is the glorification, with its perfections.

(8)

1. Prophecies concerning the Christ were made.
2. Prophecies concerning the Christ were fulfilled.
3. Prophecies concerning the Christ were realized.

(9)

1. We have a man and his wife.
2. We have Jesus and his followers.
3. We have the husband, "Christ," and the bride, "His Church."

THREE GARDENS IN CONTRAST.

	FIRST GARDEN. Text—Gen. ii. 15.	SECOND GARDEN. John xix. 14.	THIRD GARDEN. Rev. ii. 7.
1	Man.	God.	Saints.
2	Life.	Death.	Immortality.
3	Disobedience.	Obedience.	Reward of Obedience.
4	Pleasure.	Disgust.	Joys Unspeakable.
5	Forfeited.	Regained.	Enjoyed.
6	Dead Soul.	Dead Body.	Reunion of Body and Soul.
7	Fall.	Restoration.	Glorification.
8	Prophecies are Made.	Fulfilled.	Realized.
9	Man and Wife.	Jesus and Followers.	Husband and Wife.

D. McCall.

XLIII.—ELIJAH, THE TISHBITE.

CIRCUMSTANCES MAKING THIS MAN.	ELIJAH	The **MAN** The **M**ISSION The **M**ESSAGE — What { The Tishbite / To King Ahab. / From God. / Quiet, earnest, true. **M**INISTRY At Cherith. { Obedient to the command of God. / Protected and fed by the hand of God. Residing in Zarephath. { Living with a poor widow. / Sustained by a miracle.
THE KINGDOM OF ISRAEL AT THIS TIME WAS IN BAD CONDITION.	IT WAS SUFFERING UNDER THE BONDAGE OF [1] Ahab. A man of great genius, but no strength of character and moral purpose. [2] Inherited tendencies. Eight kings had led the way for Israel into idolatry and sin. [3] A heathen queen. Jezebel, licentious, reckless and idolatrous. [4] Ahab's iron rule. All the worshipers of Jehovah were sentenced to death.	
DESCRIBE THE BAAL WORSHIP.	Its { Worship. / Origin. / Introduction to Israel. / Characteristics.	Notice the { Folly. / Self-tortures of idolatry. / Uselessness.
CONTRAST THE BEARING OF THE PROPHETS OF BAAL WITH THAT OF THE PROPHET ELIJAH.	The prophets of Baal { Excited. / In mad frenzy. / Angry, but not fearless. / Filled with dismay. ELIJAH { Calm. / Dignified. / Courageous. / Filled with faith. / Challenges the prophets of Baal. / Builds an altar unto the Lord. / God hears the prayer and the people return.	
CONTRAST ELIJAH'S CONDUCT ON CARMEL WITH HIS AFTER LIFE.	**F**leeing from death / Fainting under a tree. / Fed by an angel. / Fault-finding in a cave. / Finding God on Horeb. / Furnished with God's commands.	
LESSON FROM ELIJAH'S LIFE	[1] Elijah stands as a pattern for us in decision, courage, faith and prayer. [2] Each one faces the question, Christ or the world, which? [3] Indecision here is worse than folly. [4] God to-day does not send fire, but the evidences are in the transforming of nations, families and individuals. [5] The power of one life, Elijah's, brought about a national repentance. [6] The greatest saints and heroes have seasons of deep spiritual depression. Vers. 1–3. [7] Spiritual depression often comes as the reaction from the lofty heights of spiritual power and inspiration. Vers. 1–3. [8] God's remedy for spiritual depression is work for his cause. Vers. 15, 16.	

XLIV.—CHAIN OF LIFE.

Human life has often been represented as a chain composed of various links. These links in the diagram cover a decade of life, and are indicated by the names on each link.

In the first ten years, man learns more that is of practical service than all the rest of his life. He learns to think, talk, eat and walk. He becomes familiar with nature's great laws for his physical being and well-being.

In the second decade, he begins to unfold some of the buds of mental and moral being and well-being. In the third, he forms the principles upon which the rest of his life rests. In the forth, he is at the growing prime; and in the fifth, he is at the zenith of physical power. At fifty he is at the zenith of mental and moral manhood. Then comes the waning period, ending with the sod.

Below we give an extract from a lecture on chains that will be helpful in using the diagram. It is from the pen of Prof. L. N. Fowler, of New York :

" As a chain may be strong or weak, long or short, made of good and bad links, get rusty, lost, or broken, used for a good or bad purpose—so may the chain of life.

" As a chain may be rough or smooth, bright and dark in spots, and wear most in spots—so in the chain of life.

" As a chain may be joined, welded by heat, so two lives may be joined and blended by love—the magnet will attract and hold together; a little magnet draws and holds but little.

" As the chain is perfect in proportion to the perfection of each link and the union with its fellow, so the chain of life is perfect in proportion to the perfection of each mental power and its action with all other mental powers.

"As chains become mixed up, become snarled, the links deranged, and twisted out of place, so in the chain of life, in business, courtship, marriage and health, matters get crooked, mixed up, and in confusion.

"Swivels are necessary to let the twist out of a chain when the log rolls ; it is composed of two parts, the one working within the other, and no chain is perfect without a swivel. Twists and snarls in the chain of life are produced by gambling, idleness, bad planning and circumstances, too hard work, intemperance ; and a mental swivel, made up of Causality, Constructiveness and Conscientiousness, is needed to get the kinks and snarls out.

" One chain is a thousand times more useful than another—one holds a watch, another a furious beast, and a third holds a ship with a preciouscargo and many hundred lives—so in life. Some lives are very responsible and do the most important work involving the well-being of thousands. One anchor chain will make many thousand small chains. As a violent jerk on a chain would break it, when the same amount of strain applied steadily would not break it, so a sudden shock to the mind or a violent strain on the constitution would snap both, etc.

" Chains made of jet are very tender and brittle, but will receive a high polish, are made to shine, and are more worn for ornaments than for use ; so many receive a high educational polish, are mere ornaments in high society, and are remarkably brittle and tender in the rough paths of life.

" Some chains are not what they appear to be, for they are glazed, painted or plated—so in the chain of life many externally are better or worse than they appear to be. It is not every one who can bear a close examination.

"Strings will tie together the broken links, *but* they will break. Toggles are the best for the purpose, although inconvenient and bungling. Imperfect actions, perverted appetites, broken limbs, unwise marriages, and a bad reputation, are very inconvenient, and require much toggling. The lives of some are more toggle than chains.

" It takes time and many appliances to bring some chains to their bearings, but they do a mighty work when once in their place, for they hold a powerful and costly ship in a fierce gale. So in life, it takes great and powerful influences for some men to take a certain direction, but when it is taken they carry everything they take hold of. For instance, Wilberforce, Lincoln, Oliver Cromwell, Alfred the Great, and many others.

"The dog chain is used to keep the unruly animal in a safe place. So the lives of some men are like this chain to keep the dangerous and criminial class in their place.

"As the watch chain is very handy—light, neat, available, useful and serves a good purpose—so many lives are made very handy, useful, and available for good purposes by their high tone, refined spirit, and willing, sympathetic disposition.

"A safety chain is of secondary use in securing an article more valuable than itself. So some lives are spent in looking after some other lives more important.

"Ornamental chains show how expensive and artificial a life can be made, and at the same time of how little use they are to society.

"As many chains are made to do very dirty work and left to rust for want of care, so many a life is spent in doing the hardest and dirtiest kind of work with poor pay and no thanks.

"Some chains of life are made up of broken promises, flirtation, following the fashions, failures in business, etc., while others are continually doing good, setting good examples, reforming and educating others.

"A chain with all its hooks, links, swivels, and rings is not made all at once; every part has to be made separately, and then put together piece to piece. So it takes a whole life to make a life chain; every day adds a link until the end comes.

"Let us examine our life chain as we go along."

BIRTH
CRADLE
INFANTILE INNOCENCE
(10) TENDER TENS
(20) TEACHABLE TWENTIES
(30) TIRELESS THIRTIES
(40) FIRERY FORTIES
(50) FORCIBLE FIFTIES
(60) SERIOUS SIXTIES
(70) SACRED SEVENTIES
(80) ACHING EIGHTIES
(90) SHORT'NING BREATH
(100) DEATH
THE SOD
GOD

THE CHAIN OF LIFE.

THE HAND OF DELIVERANCE IN THE BIBLE.

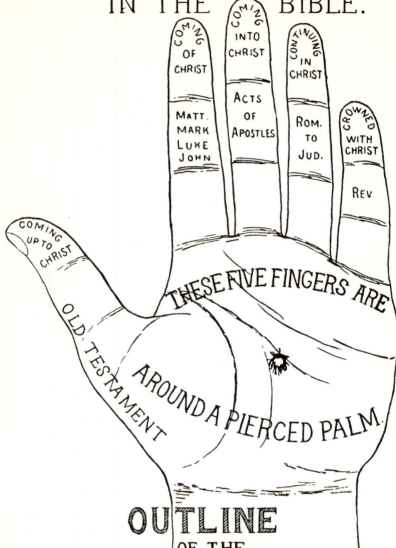

COMING OF CHRIST

MATT. MARK LUKE JOHN

COMING INTO CHRIST

ACTS OF APOSTLES

CONTINUING IN CHRIST

ROM. TO JUD.

CROWNED WITH CHRIST

REV

COMING UP TO CHRIST

OLD TESTAMENT

THESE FIVE FINGERS ARE

AROUND A PIERCED PALM.

OUTLINE OF THE HOLY SCRIPTURES.

C. B. NEWNAN

XLVI.—HOW TO READ THE BIBLE.

MOST of the books in our libraries are dead books. Our text-books in science, all our text-books, have to be revised every five years. An old edition is worthless, is misleading; to the paper-makers with it! What we regarded as fixed principles in political economy, which we learned of Adam Smith or John Stuart Mill, and supposed to be settled, are now all reversed or all modified. Sciences, arts, change. There is nothing so worthless as an old encyclopedia. It needs an appendix every year. Even in the latest "Britannica," if we look up a word like "Australia" in the early volumes of nearly twenty years ago, we are only misled. The book is dead, and the living world has left it behind.

There are a few books which it would seem can never die. The "Iliad" lives, and so does Plato's "Apology," or Shakespeare's "Hamlet." What gives them their value is not temporary, but permanent. Such books are very, very few. There are many that can live, like a blossom, for a week, or, like a fruit, for a season, and some few that will live, like a tree, for a generation; but those that can traverse the generations, passing from one to another, equally vital for each, are the choicest treasures earth has acquired. They can be numbered on one's fingers.

But even these show, generally, a decreasing vitality. When they pass from one language to another, they lose half their life. Homer is not to us what he was to the Greeks. There are but few of our people now that are interested in the wrath of Achilles or the fate of Priam's son. It is only the literary man that reads his Æneid, and he, very likely, has never read it since his student youth. Plato is only a name for most intelligent men. We may say Plato lives, but to most men it is but a thin and shadowy life. The undying book of language, the Homer, Virgil, Plato, Goethe, Shakespeare, lives for that language only; it is a dead book for nearly all the rest of the world.

But there is one Book—or shall we say one little library of books?—which we bind in one cover, in part older than the oldest,

which is the youngest and most alive of all the books ever written. Nor is it the book of one language only; but into whatever
language it is translated—and it has been translated into all—its
freshness and vitality are not in the least diminished. The generations go by, and the sciences are born and re-born again and again,
but they do not make that book obsolete. It was a book of power
in its youth, when it was produced, part by part; and it is a book
to-day of vastly more power, of constantly growing power; a tree
fresher ever, and broader, stronger and ever strengthening, under
whose shadows the nations of the earth do rest, whose leaves are
their healing, and whose fruit is their sustenance.

HOW TO TAKE PROFIT IN READING OF THE HOLY SCRIPTURE.

Whosoever mindeth to take profit by reading Scriptures, must

1　Earnestly and usually pray unto God that he will vouchsafe to
- Teach the way of his statutes.
- Give understanding.
- Direct in the path of his commandments.

Psa. cxix.

2　Diligently keep such order of reading the Scriptures and prayer as may stand with his calling and state of life, so that
- At the least, twice every day this exercise be kept. — Deut. xi. 10.
- The time once appointed hereunto after a good entry, be no otherwise employed. — Luke ix. 62.
- Superstition be avoided.
- At one other time that be done, which is left undone at any time. — Esa. 29:36. Eph. 5:16.

3　Understand to what end and purpose the Scriptures serve, which were written to
- Teach, that we may learn truth.
- Improve, that we may be kept from error.
- Correct, that we may be driven from vice. — II. Tim. iii. 16, 17.
- Instruct, that we may be settled in the way of well-doing.
- Comfort, that in trouble we may be confirmed in patient hope. — Rom. xv. 4.

4　Remember that the Scriptures contain matter concerning

Religion and the right worshipping of God, as
- Faith in one God { Father. Son. Holy Ghost.
- The state of mankind, by { 1. Creation. 2. Fall and sin. 3. Regeneration in Christ.
- The government thereof { Before Christ. Since Christ.
- The word of God written in the Testament. { O d. New.
- Sacraments { Before Christ. Since Christ.
- The end and general judgment of the { Good. Wicked.

Commonwealths and governments of people, by
- Magistrates { Good. Evil.
- Peace and war.
- Prosperity and plagues.
- Subjects { Quiet. Disordered.

Families and things that belong to household, in which are { Husbands. Wives. Parents. Children. Masters. Servants. } Godly blessed. Ungodly plagued.

The private life and doings of every man in
- Wisdom and folly.
- Love and hatred.
- Soberness and incontinence.
- Mirth and sorrow.
- Speech and silence.
- Pride and humility.
- Covetousness and liberality.

The common life of all men, as
- Riches, poverty.
- Nobility.
- Favor.
- Labor and idleness.

5　Refuse all sense of Scripture contrary to the { Plain teaching of other passages. General tenor of Bible truth.

6　Mark and consider the
- 1. Coherence of the text, how it hangeth together.
- 2. Course of times and ages, with such things as belong unto them.
- 3. Manner of speech proper to the Scriptures.
- 4. Agreement that one place of Scripture hath with another, whereby that which seemeth dark in one is made easy in the other.

7　Take opportunity to
- Read interpreters if he be able.
- Confer with such as can open the Scriptures. Acts viii. 30, 31, etc.
- Hear preaching, and to prove by the Scriptures that which is taught. Acts xvii. 13.

XLVII.—THE ROAD TO HEAVEN.

LARGE circle represents the earth as distinguished from Heaven. Large circle No. 2 represents Heaven, the traveler's goal, and it is mostly hidden from us. Small circle No. 1 represents the world as distinguished from the church, and small circle No. 2 the church between the world and Heaven. A is the road to Heaven, and B is the path by which wanderers return.

I. The Road.—1. Begins on earth; 2. Is an upward road; and, 3, is made up of successive steps.

> " Heaven is not reached at a single bound.
> We build the ladder by which we climb
> From lowly earth to heights sublime,
> And mount it round by round."

II. The Sinner.—1. Begins with hearing and proceeds with belief; 2. Repentance; and, 3, confession, but is still in the world; the next step of surrender, Baptism, is the God-selected place of pardon and adoption. The sinner there puts on Christ—becomes a Christian. References: 1. Rom. x. 13, 14. 2. Acts xvi. 31. 3. Acts xvii. 30. 4. Rom. x. 10. 5. Gal. iii. 27; Rom. vi. 4; I. Pet. iii. 21.

III. The Christian is only well started now; Virtue or Courage will be needed next; then follow successively: 2. Knowledge; 3. Temperance; 4. Patience; 5. Godliness; 6. Brotherly kindness, and finally, as the climax of all, the crowning virtue of all, 7. Love, which admits to heaven. II. Pet. i. 5–7. Should the Christian go astray, he has a way of return: 1. Repentance; 2. Confession; 3. Prayer. Acts viii. 22; I. John ii. 14.

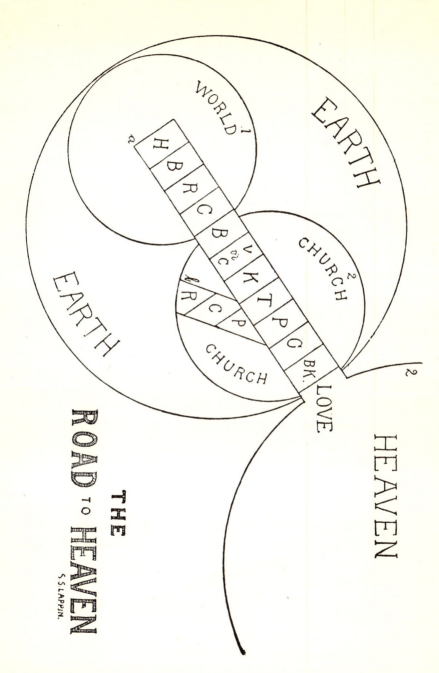

THE
ROAD TO HEAVEN
S. S. LAPPIN.

XLVIII.—-THE LIFE OF PAUL.

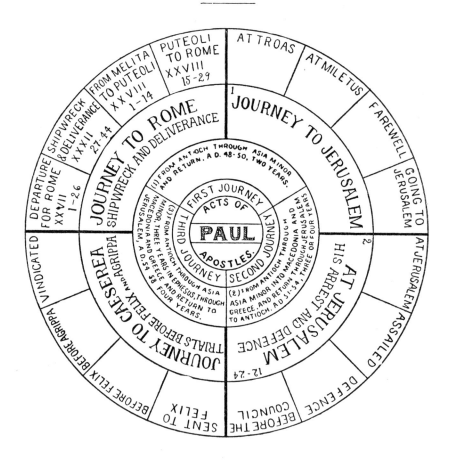